HOW TO BE VEGAN AND KEEP YOUR FRIENDS

Recipes by Annie Nichols

Additional text by Quadrille

PHOTOGRAPHY BY KIM LIGHTBODY

quadrille

Vegan, your way

〰〰〰〰〰〰〰〰〰〰〰〰〰〰〰〰〰〰〰〰〰〰〰〰〰〰〰〰

There are millions of vegans around the world, yet no two are alike. Not only do their diets vary, but also their take on veganism – from ethical, environmental and/or political, to a straightforward preference for plant-based food.

The Vegan Society in England established the term 'vegan' in 1944 by amalgamating the first and last letters of the word 'vegetarian' and deleting the bits in between (how apt). Over the years it has refined its definition for the lifestyle choice. Today, it reads:

'A philosophy and way of living which seeks to exclude – as far as is possible and practicable – all forms of exploitation of, and cruelty to, animals for food, clothing or any other purpose; and by extension, promotes the development and use of animal-free alternatives for the benefit of humans, animals and the environment. In dietary terms it denotes the practice of dispensing with all products derived wholly or partly from animals.'

Like any philosophy, it is open to interpretation. So the first rule of being vegan and keeping your friends is: there are no rules. There is no one way; there is no right way. Be true to you. Do veganism the way you choose to.

Consider this book a kitchen tool to help you cook food that is delicious, shareable, snackable and devoid of 'sacrifice'. Some recipes are simple, others push you to find unusual ingredients and dishes that break from the vegan norm. It is also an inspiration for living vegan and happy, from eating out in a world of carnivores to having pals over for dinner; tips are scattered throughout.

Your options should open up, you'll enjoy a whole new menu of food, and your friends... well, they'll never have a bad word to say again!

Almond & Mango Bars

MAKES 16 BARS

2 tbsp coconut oil

50g / ¼ cup molasses sugar, muscovado or dark brown sugar

4 tbsp maple, date or rice syrup

200g / 7oz canned mango slices in juice (drained weight), mashed, or 1 fresh ripe mango, peeled, stoned and mashed

100g / 1¼ cups flaked (slivered) almonds

200g / 2 cups rolled oats

100g / ¾ cup black and white poppy seeds

50g / 6 tbsp sesame seeds

50g / 6 tbsp flaxseeds

juice of ½ lemon

75g / 2⅔oz dried mango, snipped into small pieces

50g / 1¾oz coconut chips or desiccated (dried shredded) coconut

pinch of salt

Preheat the oven to 160°C / 320°F / gas mark 3. Grease and line a 22 x 32cm / 8½ x 12½in baking tin (pan) with parchment paper.

Place the coconut oil, sugar, syrup and mashed mango into a large pan over a low heat, stirring until melted. Add the remaining ingredients and stir until well combined.

Scrape the mixture into the prepared baking tin and spread out evenly using the back of a spoon or a spatula. Bake for 30–35 minutes, or until golden.

Leave the mixture to cool for 5 minutes in the baking tin. While it is still warm, mark it into 16 rectangular bars, scoring lines with a knife. Then remove from the tin to a wire rack to cool. When completely cold, break into bars.

Store in an airtight container for up to a week.

These bars are great for an on-the-go breakfast or afternoon snack. Be flexible with the ingredients – for example, try camelina, sunflower or pumpkin seeds. They all give good crunch!

Cacao, Banana & Brazil Nut Bars

MAKES 16 BARS

50g / 3½ tbsp coconut oil

50g / 4 tbsp dark muscovado sugar or coconut sugar

3 tbsp maple, rice or agave syrup

120g / ½ cup nut butter (almond, hazelnut or peanut)

50g / ½ cup cacao nibs

1 tsp vanilla paste

2 ripe bananas, mashed

50g / ⅓ cup sunflower or pumpkin seeds, or a mixture of both

150g / 1½ cups rolled oats

100g / ¾ cup Brazil nuts, roughly chopped

finely grated zest and juice of 1 orange

50g / ½ cup raw cacao powder

pinch of salt

Preheat the oven to 160°C / 320°F / gas mark 3. Grease and line a 22 x 32cm / 8½ x 12½in baking tin (pan) with parchment paper.

Place the coconut oil, sugar, syrup, nut butter, cacao nibs and vanilla paste into a large pan over a low-medium heat. Stir until the sugar has dissolved, then remove from the heat, add the rest of the ingredients and mix well.

Scrape the mixture into the prepared baking tin and level the top with a spatula. Bake for 20–25 minutes, until golden brown.

Leave the mixture to cool for 5 minutes in the baking tin. While it is still warm, mark it into 16 rectangular bars by scoring lines with a knife. Then remove from the tin to a wire rack to cool. When completely cold, break into bars.

Store in an airtight container for up to a week.

Strawberry Bircher

SERVES 4

MUESLI

200g / 2 cups rolled oats,
   jumbo oats or porridge oats
600ml / 2½ cups nut milk,
   oat milk or soya milk
juice of 1 lemon
4 prunes, stoned and finely
   chopped
50g / ⅓ cup dried cherries
   or blueberries
2½ tbsp ground flaxseeds
50g / ⅓ cup sunflower seeds
2 tbsp dark brown or
   muscovado sugar

STRAWBERRIES

200g / 7oz strawberries
50g / ¼ cup coconut sugar
   or light brown sugar
pinch of sea salt flakes
pinch of freshly ground
   black pepper

If using rolled oats or jumbo oats, you'll need to soak this breakfast overnight. But if you want to make this on the day, use porridge oats.

Stir all the ingredients for the muesli together in a bowl. If using rolled or jumbo oats, cover and refrigerate overnight. If using porridge oats, cover and refrigerate for 10 minutes.

To serve, slice the strawberries into a bowl, sprinkle with the sugar, salt and pepper, toss together and set aside for 15 minutes.

Remove the muesli from the fridge, spoon into bowls and serve each one topped with a spoonful of the strawberries.

Get yourself a couple of coconuts and make your own rich and creamy milk – you'll never go back to cartons again.

Fresh Coconut Milk

MAKES ABOUT 400ML / 14FL OZ

2 mature (brown) coconuts

Preheat the oven to 200°C / 400°F / gas mark 6.

Drain the water out of each of the coconuts by piercing the two soft eyes on the coconut shell. Reserve the water either to drink, or you can add it to the first pressing, later.

Place the coconuts in the oven for 20–30 minutes. This will cause the shell to crack and make them easier to break open.

Allow to cool a little and then, holding the coconut in a cloth, use something heavy like a hammer to crack it open. Opening it this way allows you to get the flesh out easily. Repeat with the other coconut.

Remove all of the coconut shell and discard. Break the pieces of coconut flesh into the jug of a blender or food processor. Add about 300ml / 1¼ cups warm water (or the reserved coconut water) and whizz until smooth.

Pour the coconut mixture through a sieve (strainer) lined with a piece of muslin (cheesecloth), then gather up the cloth and squeeze out the milk into a jug (pitcher) or bowl. This first pressing should be rich and creamy.

Place the leftover coconut, still wrapped in its muslin, in a bowl of warm water and leave to soak for an hour, then squeeze the muslin again over another jug or bowl to extract a second pressing of milk.

The first pressing is better used for cooking as it is much richer and creamier; the second pressing is really good to drink. You can keep the milks separate or mix together.

Place the coconut milk in fridge until chilled. It will keep for 4–5 days.

Fruity Maca Energy Bombs

MAKES 12

100g / 1½ cup dried
  barberries
125g / 1 cup cashews
50g / 3½ tbsp tahini (sesame
  paste)
75g / ½ cup prunes
100ml / 7 tbsp maple, date
  or rice syrup
½ tsp vanilla extract or paste
2 tsp maca powder, optional
4 tbsp sesame seeds
pinch of ground cinnamon

**Maca has a kind of
malty taste and
barberries are quite
sharp. If you can't
find barberries (often
stocked at Middle
Eastern grocers) use
chopped up dried
cranberries or cherries.**

Put all of the ingredients into the bowl of a food processor
and whizz for about a minute, or until the mixture is very
finely chopped and starting to come together in a mass.

Refrigerate the mixture for 1 hour to firm up a bit and
make rolling easier.

Remove from the fridge. Use your hands to roll the
mixture into 12 walnut-sized balls. If the mixture is too
sticky, it may be easier to roll with slightly wet hands.

Place the bombs in a sealed, airtight container and
refrigerate. The bombs will keep in the refrigerator
for up to a week.

Matcha & Hemp Balls

MAKES 16 BALLS

175g / 1¼ cups peas, fresh or
  frozen (defrosted if frozen)
175g / 1¼ cups edamame
  (soy beans), frozen
50g / ½ cup rolled oats
3 tbsp nut butter (peanut,
  almond or cashew)
3 tbsp hulled hemp seeds
1–2 tbsp matcha powder
juice of ½–1 lemon
6 tbsp white or black sesame
  seeds
1½–3 tbsp coconut oil, if
  frying, or a little for
  greasing
sea salt and freshly ground
  black pepper

These have a very 'green' savoury taste and the result is soft (rather than firm) balls.

Blanch the peas and beans in lightly salted boiling water for 3–5 minutes, until just tender, then drain.

While still warm, tip the drained peas and beans into the bowl of a food processor. Add the oats, nut butter, hemp seeds and the matcha powder. Squeeze in the juice of half a lemon and whizz until puréed. The mixture should hold together when squeezed with your fingers.

Scrape into a bowl and season with salt and pepper and more lemon juice to taste. Divide the mixture into 16 even-sized pieces and roll into balls. Put the sesame seeds onto a plate, then roll the balls into the sesame seeds, coating all over. At this point, you can freeze the balls to cook much later, or store in an airtight container until ready to cook when needed.

When ready to cook, the balls can be fried in coconut oil or baked. To fry, heat a large frying pan over a high heat, add about 1½ tablespoons of coconut oil and once melted, add the balls to the pan and cook until lightly golden all over (you may need to do this in batches, adding more oil to the pan halfway through).

To bake, preheat the oven to 180°C / 360°F / gas mark 4 and place the balls on a lightly greased baking tray. Bake for about 20–25 minutes or until lightly crispy.

The cooked balls will keep for 4–5 days in the refrigerator.

Green Tea Noodles

SERVES 4–6

NOODLES

150g / 1 heaped cup 00
  grade flour
210g / 1½ cups plain (all-
  purpose) flour, plus a little
  extra for dusting
3 tbsp matcha powder

BROTH

5cm / 2in piece fresh root
  ginger, finely grated
2 cloves garlic, crushed with
  a pinch of salt
1 tbsp Shaoxing rice wine
  or sherry
¼ tsp freshly ground
  white pepper
2 star anise
1 cinnamon stick

pinch of chilli flakes
1 tbsp Sichuan peppercorns
  (optional)
6 spring onions (scallions)
6 tbsp loose green tea
3 tbsp sesame oil
3 tbsp dark soy sauce
200g / 7oz green leaves (baby
  spinach or small leaves of
  pak choi / bok choy),
  roughly chopped
350g / 12oz edamame (soy
  beans), peas or skinned
  broad (fava) beans,
  defrosted if frozen
1 tbsp black sesame seeds
wasabi paste (optional)
salt and freshly ground
  black pepper

**A nutritious noodle
breakfast (with a gentle
hit of caffeine) is a
hearty way to start
the day.**

To make the green tea noodles, mix together the flours
and matcha in a large bowl until evenly combined. Pour
in 200–225ml / 6¾–7½fl oz water, or enough to bring
everything together to form a soft, but firm dough. Scrape
onto a work surface and knead for about 10 minutes until
smooth. Cover with the bowl and allow to rest for an hour.

Cut the dough into four and use a pasta machine to roll
out each piece very thinly. Alternatively roll out as thinly
as possible on a lightly floured work surface using a
rolling pin. >>>

>>> Using a sharp knife, or pasta machine, slice into 1cm / ½in wide noodles and toss in a little flour. If not using immediately, hang the noodles over a clean, floured broom handle (horizontally positioned) until ready to use.

To make the broth, pour 1½ litres / 6½ cups water into a large pan. Add the ginger, garlic, rice wine, white pepper, star anise, cinnamon, chilli and Sichuan peppercorns, if using. Cut the green parts off the spring onions (scallions) and add to the pot. Finely slice the whites of the spring onions and set aside.

Bring to the boil, then remove from the heat and stir in the tea leaves. Cover and leave to steep for 30 minutes, then strain through a fine sieve (strainer) into a clean pan.

Bring the broth to the boil. Add a pinch of salt, stir in the noodles, return to a boil again and cook the noodles until tender.

Hook out the noodles with tongs into a large bowl, toss with a tablespoon of sesame oil and set aside.

Add the remaining sesame oil and the soy sauce to the broth, then simmer gently for 5–10 minutes.

Taste the broth for seasoning and adjust if necessary. Stir in your choice of green leaves, edamame (soy beans), peas or broad beans (fava beans) and the spring onion whites and simmer for a few minutes more or until the leaves are just tender.

Divide the noodles between 4–6 serving bowls. Ladle over the hot broth and vegetables. Serve sprinkled with the sesame seeds, and stir in a little wasabi, if you like.

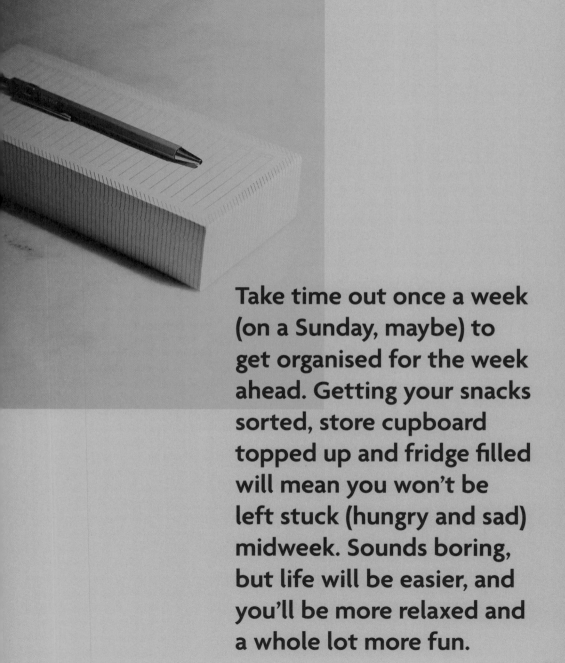

Take time out once a week (on a Sunday, maybe) to get organised for the week ahead. Getting your snacks sorted, store cupboard topped up and fridge filled will mean you won't be left stuck (hungry and sad) midweek. Sounds boring, but life will be easier, and you'll be more relaxed and a whole lot more fun.

Aloo Tikki
/ Herby Walnut Chutney

**MAKES 6 LARGE OR 18
SMALL PATTIES**

ALOO TIKKI

2–3 floury potatoes, such as
  Maris Piper (about 500g /
  17½oz)

3 tbsp rice flour, plus extra
  for dusting

2 tbsp coconut oil, plus more
  for frying the patties

1 tsp cumin seeds

1½ tsp black onion seeds

12 curry leaves or 2 tbsp
  chopped fresh coriander
  (cilantro)

1 onion, finely chopped

1 green chilli, deseeded and
  finely chopped

6cm / 2½in piece fresh root
  ginger, finely grated

2 cloves garlic, crushed

½ tsp garam masala

1 tsp salt

juice of ½ lemon

25g / ⅓ cup unsweetened
  desiccated (dried shredded)
  coconut, or 125g / 4½oz
  fresh coconut, grated

100g / ⅔ cup peas, fresh or
  frozen (defrosted if frozen)

CHUTNEY

3 tbsp walnut halves, lightly
  toasted and chopped

4 tbsp finely chopped fresh
  coriander (cilantro)

2 tbsp chopped fresh mint

1 green chilli, deseeded and
  finely chopped

1 clove garlic, crushed

3cm / 1in piece fresh root
  ginger, very finely grated

pinch of salt

1 tbsp lemon or lime juice

**This Indian street food
snack – a sort of potato
fritter – is an exciting,
spice-filled brunch.
Alternatively, wait until
the end of the day and
pair with a cold beer.**

Preheat the oven to 200°C / 400°F / gas mark 6.

Prick each of the potatoes two or three times with a fork
and bake in the oven for about 45 minutes–1 hour or
until tender. (Or peel and quarter, then boil the potatoes
in lightly salted water, until tender.) >>>

>>> While the potatoes are cooking, make the chutney. Stir all the ingredients for the chutney together in a small bowl, adding a little water to loosen the mix. Set aside.

When the potatoes are cooked and cool enough to handle, peel off the skin, drop the flesh into a large bowl and mash well. (You should have about 350g / 12oz of mash.) Beat the rice flour into the potato mash, little by little, so that the mixture forms a dough.

Heat the coconut oil in a pan. Add the cumin seeds, onion seeds and curry leaves or coriander (cilantro) and fry for 1–2 minutes, or until the curry leaves crackle. Add the chopped onion and chilli and cook for 8–10 minutes until softened without colour.

Add the ginger, garlic and garam masala and cook for a couple more minutes. Stir in the salt, lemon juice and coconut, then scoop the contents of the pan into the potato dough and mix together well. Tip the peas into the still-hot pan, and stir fry for a few minutes, until just tender. Remove from the heat and set aside.

Divide the potato dough into 6 large patties or 18 small patties and, with floured hands, take one piece at a time in the palm of your hand and press out into a flat round. Scoop some of the peas into the centre of each round and bring the edges of the dough together, over the peas, to seal. Dust the patty with a little more rice flour, set aside, then repeat with the remaining mixture.

Heat a frying pan over a medium heat, add ½ tablespoon coconut oil. When the oil is melted, slide in a few of the patties and cook for 3–4 minutes, until the bases are lightly golden, then turn over and cook on the other sides for another 3–4 minutes. Continue to cook in batches.

Serve warm with the chutney.

Coconut oil is slightly sweet, usually available in solid form and can be used as an alternative to butter and other oils in cooking as it has a high melting point. It can taste a bit coconutty and overpower more delicate dishes. Coconut butter, on the other hand, can be almost flavourless.

Aubergine & Potato Patties / Sweetcorn 'Polenta'

MAKES 12 LITTLE PATTIES

PATTIES

1 large potato (about 350g / 12oz)

2 large aubergines (eggplants), chopped into 4cm / 1½in cubes

3 tbsp olive oil, plus extra for frying

400g / 14oz can chickpeas (garbanzo beans), drained and roughly mashed

1 tbsp tahini (sesame paste) (optional)

2 cloves garlic, crushed

1 tsp ground cumin

zest and juice of ½ lemon

small bunch of fresh thyme

salt and freshly ground black pepper

SWEETCORN 'POLENTA'

6 sweetcorn cobs (ears of corn)

3 tbsp extra virgin olive oil

Preheat the oven to 200°C / 400°F / gas mark 6.

Prick the potato two or three times with a fork and bake in the oven for about 45 minutes–1 hour or until tender.

At the same time, place the chopped aubergines (eggplants) in a roasting pan with 3 tbsp of the olive oil. Add a pinch of salt, toss well together and bake for about 40 minutes, stirring once or twice, until very tender.

When the potato is cooked, and cool enough to handle, peel off the skin, drop into a large bowl and mash well. (You should have about 325g / 11½oz of mash.) Add the cooked aubergine to the mashed potato in the bowl and mash well again.

Add the mashed chickpeas (garbanzo beans) to the bowl with the tahini (sesame paste), if using, and the garlic, cumin, lemon zest and juice, and 1 tablespoon of thyme leaves (pulled from the sprigs). Season and mix well, then set aside.

To make the 'polenta', cut off the very top and bottom of each corn cob. Stand each one up on one end and use a sharp knife to carefully shave off the corn kernels.

Place the corn kernels in a medium saucepan and just cover them with water. Add the oil, and simmer gently over a medium heat for 12 minutes. >>>

>>> Drain the corn, reserving the water, and drop the kernels into the bowl of a food processor. Whizz the corn until smooth, adding some of the reserved cooking liquid to help it process.

Scrape the corn paste back into the pan with the remaining cooking liquid and simmer, while stirring, over a low heat for about 10–15 minutes or until the mixture thickens to the consistency of wallpaper paste. Season and cook for a further 2 minutes. Taste and adjust the seasoning. Keep warm while you cook the patties.

Heat a tablespoon of olive oil in a large frying pan, add a few of the remaining thyme sprigs to the pan and scoop large tablespoons of the patty mix on top of the thyme. Fry the patties for 3–4 minutes on each side or until golden and cooked through. You will need do this in batches, adding more oil when necessary.

Spoon the sweetcorn 'polenta' into a serving bowl and place the patties on top (or on a serving platter) for everyone to help themselves.

Molasses Baked Beans / Smashed Peas

SERVES 6–8

250g / 1½ cups dried pinto
  or haricot beans

250g / 1½ cups dried black
  or turtle beans

50g / 4 tbsp molasses sugar
  or soft dark brown sugar

2 tsp ground cinnamon

3 tbsp molasses or treacle

2 tbsp English mustard
  powder

1 tsp smoked paprika

8 cloves

2 sprigs of fresh thyme

6 bay leaves

4 large onions, chopped

8 cloves garlic, crushed

2 red chillies, split
  lengthways, stalk intact

2 x 400g / 14oz cans tomatoes

2 tbsp red wine vinegar

salt and ground black pepper

SMASHED PEAS

5 tbsp olive oil

1 clove garlic, crushed

3 spring onions (scallions),
  finely chopped

150g / 1 cup peas, fresh or
  frozen (defrosted) peas

2 tbsp lemon juice

1 tbsp chopped fresh dill,
  tarragon or mint

Tip the dried beans into a large bowl, add enough water to cover and leave to soak for 8 hours or overnight. Then drain and rinse the soaked beans well, drain again and place in a large casserole dish.

Preheat oven to 150°C / 300°F / gas mark 2.

Mix together the sugar, cinnamon, molasses or treacle and mustard powder in a small bowl and add to the beans. Add all the remaining ingredients except the vinegar.

Pour 1 litre / 4½ cups water over the beans to cover, and bring to the boil, skimming off any scum that rises to the top. Cover with a tight-fitting lid and place in the oven for 3–4 hours or until the beans are tender. Check every once in a while, and if it seems dry, top up with boiling water.

Remove from the oven and stir in the vinegar. Taste and adjust the seasoning if necessary.

To make the smashed peas, heat 2 tablespoons of the oil in a pan over a medium-high heat. Add the garlic and spring onions (scallions) and cook for 2–3 minutes until softened. Add the peas, stir together, and pour over a cup of water. Cover with a lid and cook for about 3–5 minutes until the peas are tender and cooked through.

Remove the peas from heat, and mash well. Stir in the lemon juice, chopped herbs and the remaining oil and season to taste.

Serve the beans in bowls or on toast with the smashed peas on the side.

Corn Ceviche Dressing / Avocado Toast

SERVES 4

CORN CEVICHE

1 tbsp vegetable oil

1 Scotch bonnet chilli, deseeded and finely chopped

1 yellow pepper (bell pepper), deseeded and finely chopped

½ onion, finely chopped

1 small clove garlic, crushed

zest and juice of 1 small orange

juice of 2 limes

kernels sliced from 2 uncooked sweetcorn cobs (ears of corn)

1cm / ½in piece of fresh root ginger, finely grated

salt

CORIANDER OIL

leaves from a small bunch of fresh coriander (cilantro)

100ml / ⅓ cup extra virgin olive oil

TO SERVE

olive oil, for frying

4 slices of sourdough bread

2 large avocados

3 spring onions (scallions), finely sliced

To make the ceviche dressing, pour the vegetable oil into a large, heavy-based saucepan. Heat over a medium heat, then add the chopped chilli, pepper, onion, garlic and orange zest and season with a pinch of salt.

Cook over a low heat for about 5–6 minutes, or until softened. You do not want the vegetables to colour. Remove the pan from the heat and leave to cool.

Once cooled, stir in the orange and lime juices, two-thirds of the corn kernels and the grated ginger. Transfer the mixture to a food processor or blender and whizz until very smooth. Strain into a bowl, reserving the juice.

To make the coriander oil, bring a small pan of lightly salted water to the boil, add the coriander (cilantro) leaves, remove from the heat immediately, drain and refresh under cold water. Drain again, squeeze out any excess water then chop the leaves roughly and transfer to the bowl of a food processor. Pour in the oil and whizz until smooth. Scrape the herb oil out into a bowl. Set aside.

Heat a little olive oil in a large frying or griddle pan and fry the sourdough slices on both sides until golden. Place a slice of toast on each of four serving plates.

To serve, slice the avocados thinly and divide between the slices of toast. Drizzle over a little of the ceviche dressing and coriander oil.

Finally sprinkle with a few of the remaining corn kernels and the sliced spring onions (scallions).

Raw Nut Butter

MAKES 1 MEDIUM JAR

250g / 9oz nuts (cashews
  or pistachios work best)

Soak the nuts – skin on or off is up
to you – overnight in plenty of cold
water (use filtered water if you like).

The next day, drain the nuts, rinse,
drain again and tip into the bowl of
a food processor. Now whizz the nuts
until you have a creamy consistency
that you like. Whizz more if you like
a smoother butter.

Roasted Nut Butter

MAKES 1 MEDIUM JAR

250g / 9oz peanuts,
  almonds, cashews,
  Brazil nuts, macadamias,
  pistachios or hazelnuts
small spoonful of coconut,
  rapeseed (canola) or
  groundnut oil, optional

Preheat the oven to 180°C / 360°F /
gas mark 4.

Spread the nuts on a baking tray
(pan). Roast for about 6–7 minutes
(set a timer as it's easy to forget and
burn them!).

Check the nuts, shake the tray and
place back in the oven. Continue to
roast for a couple more minutes, or
until evenly golden. If you're not sure
if they're ready, chop a nut in half –
the centre should be golden. Once
roasted, tip the nuts out onto a plate
and leave to cool completely.

Tip the cooled nuts into the bowl of
a food processor and whizz, scraping
down the sides every now and then,
until the butter is as smooth as you
like. This may take 5–10 minutes,
so be patient. If you'd like a more oily
nut butter, add the coconut, rapeseed
(canola) or groundnut oil.

Making nut butter is so easy. It's cheaper than the store-bought stuff and you can make it how you like it: roast the nuts or keep them raw; sweeten with sugar or syrup, if you like; add salt or not; make it oily or dry... it's all up to you. Use these recipes as your starting point.

Oat milk is quick and easy to make and has a lovely malty flavour. Use in tea or on granola or to make lattes and smoothies.

 **Oat Milk**

For every 100g / 1 cup rolled or porridge oats pour over 750ml / 3¼ cups of water, and leave to soak for a minimum of 30 minutes. For a creamier milk, leave for 3–4 hours or even overnight.

Place a piece of muslin (cheesecloth) into a sieve (strainer) set over a large bowl and pour in the milk. Bring up the edges of the cloth and squeeze really well to remove as much milk as possible, leaving the pulp in the muslin.

Store the milk in the fridge for up to 3–4 days.

Turmeric & Mango Latte

SERVES 1

200ml / scant 1 cup almond
  or oat milk
2 tsp agave nectar, or maple
  or rice syrup
½ tsp ground turmeric
small pinch of sea salt
pinch of ground cardamom
  (optional)
½ small ripe mango, peeled,
  stoned and roughly
  chopped

**If you can get hold of
fresh turmeric, use it
in place of the ground.
Take a 4cm / 1½in
piece, scrape the skin
away with the tip of a
teaspoon, grate finely
and add to the milk in
the pan.**

Pour the milk into a small pan and add the syrup,
turmeric, salt and cardamom, if using.

Bring to just below the boil. Take off the heat, add the
chopped mango and set aside for 5 minutes.

Pour the mix into a blender or use a stick blender and
blend until smooth.

Pour into a glass and serve warm.

Almond & Chickpea Cookies

MAKES ABOUT 30 COOKIES

1 x 400g / 14oz can of
  chickpeas (garbanzo beans)
50g / ½ cup ground almonds
150g / 5oz hulled hemp seeds
½ tsp vanilla extract or paste
100g / ½ cup almond or other
  nut butter
pinch of salt
zest of 1 lemon, finely grated,
  or a small pinch of ground
  cardamom (optional)
½ tsp cream of tartar
125g / ⅔ cup golden caster
  (superfine) sugar or light
  brown sugar, plus extra for
  sprinkling
1 tsp baking powder
flaked almonds, for
  sprinkling

**Hulled hemp seeds have
a nutty, moist texture
which creates a crunchy
cookie with a slightly
chewy centre.**

Preheat the oven to 180°C / 360°F / gas mark 4 and line
two 22 x 32cm / 8½ x 12½in baking trays (pans) with
parchment paper.

Drain the chickpeas (garbanzo beans), reserving the
water, and tip them into the bowl of a food processor. Add
the ground almonds, hemp seeds, vanilla, nut butter and
salt and whizz until very smooth. Scrape out into a bowl
and stir in the lemon zest or cardamom, if using.

Pour the reserved water drained from the chickpeas into
a large bowl and use an electric hand-whisk or stand
mixer to whisk for approximately 5 minutes until it has
more than doubled in size, and is white and foamy.

Add the cream of tartar and whisk again for another
minute. Slowly add the sugar, whisking until the mixture
forms stiff, glossy peaks.

Beat the baking powder into the chickpea and almond
mixture then beat in one-third of the meringue. Carefully
fold in the rest of the meringue. Scoop out tablespoonfuls
of the mixture onto the lined baking trays, allowing space
for the cookies to spread.

Sprinkle the cookies generously with flaked almonds and
a little extra sugar. Bake for 20–25 minutes or until lightly
golden. Remove from the oven. (When they come out
of the oven, you can use a fancy cookie cutter to cut out
neater shapes. Eat the trimmings as you go!) Allow to cool
a little on the trays, then cool completely on a wire rack.

Store in an airtight container for up to 4–5 days.

Almond Milk

MAKES ABOUT 750ML /
25FL OZ

300g / 2¼ cups almonds (you
can use other shelled nuts if
you prefer)

**You can also make nut
milk ice cubes: freeze
fresh nut milk in ice-
cube trays. Once solid,
pop out the cubes, place
in a zip-lock bag and
return to the freezer.
The creamy cubes can
be added to smoothies.**

**No time to make fresh
nut milk? Whip up a
cheat's version: add
a few tablespoons of
nut butter to some
chilled water and whizz
in a blender until silky.
Strain if you like it
super smooth.**

Tip the almonds into a large bowl
and pour over enough water to cover.
Leave to soak for at least 8–12 hours
(or up to 2–3 days). The longer you
soak the nuts, the easier they will be
to blend, and the creamier the milk
will be.

Drain and rinse the almonds. If the
nuts have skin on, pop them out
of their skins and discard. Or you
can leave them on, if you prefer.
(Removing the almond skins yields a
lighter-coloured milk.)

Measure 1.2 litres / 5 cups of cold
water. Drop the almonds into
the jug of a blender or bowl of a
food processor.

Pour in some of the measured water
to cover the nuts and whizz at the
highest speed, adding more water if
needed, until very smooth, white and
frothy. You might not need all of the
water. Simply reach the consistency
you like.

Place a piece of muslin (cheesecloth)
into a sieve (strainer) set over a bowl
and pour in the milk. Bring up the
edges of the cloth and squeeze really
well to remove as much milk as you
can, leaving the pulp in the muslin.

Store the milk in the fridge for up to
3–4 days. >>>

>>> You'll be left with a bag of nut pulp. You can use this in smoothies, energy bars or balls (you can freeze it at this point if you don't want to use it immediately).

Alternatively, to make almond meal, spread evenly onto a baking tray and place in an oven – preheated to 120°C / 250°F / gas mark ½ – for about an hour, stirring occasionally, or until completely dry, then store in an airtight container. You can use this in cakes and biscuits.

Ever lamented the price of a tiny packet of nuts? Leave the supermarket behind and head to international/ independent grocery stores. You can score big bags of nuts for less. Same goes for buying spices, fresh herbs and pulses. Browse the aisles and you might even discover new-to-you foods and ingredients. Bonus.

Ginger Tofu Rice Balls / Passion Fruit Dressing

MAKES ABOUT 50 BALLS

RICE BALLS

½ quantity Sushi Rice
(page 97)

300g / 10½oz firm tofu
(beancurd)

6 spring onions (scallions),
finely chopped

5cm / 2in piece fresh root
ginger, finely grated, or
15g / ½oz pickled ginger

2 cloves garlic, crushed

2 tbsp white miso paste

edamame (soy beans)
(optional)

vegetable oil, for frying

salt and freshly ground
black pepper

PASSION FRUIT DRESSING

6 passion fruits

3½ tbsp light soy sauce

1 tbsp mirin

½ tsp wasabi

few fresh mint leaves, finely
shredded

2 tsp sesame oil

1 tsp soft brown sugar

marigold petals (optional)

Marigold (*Calendula officinalis*) petals are not only vibrant in colour, they also give a kick of a light peppery flavour. These are perfect as nibbles for a party with drinks, especially for a brunch or lunch. You could also press an edamame bean into the centre of each rice ball before rolling.

Make the Sushi Rice (page 97) and while it is still warm, crumble in the tofu (beancurd), and add the spring onions (scallions), ginger, garlic and miso paste. Season to taste, then mix well to combine.

Using wet hands, roll the mixture into little balls the size of a walnut. Press an edamame (soy bean) in the middle of the balls, if you like. Place the balls on a tray, put in the fridge and leave to chill while you make the dressing.

Cut each passion fruit in half and, using a teaspoon, scoop out the flesh into a bowl. Add 1 tablespoon water and the rest of the ingredients, apart from the marigold petals, and stir well to dissolve the sugar, adding a pinch of black pepper. Scatter over the marigold petals, then set aside.

Heat a large frying pan, add 2 tablespoons of vegetable oil, then add a few of the chilled rice balls (you'll need to do this in batches, adding more oil if needed), and cook for 5–8 minutes, rolling them around the pan every now and then, until golden and heated through. Scoop the balls out onto a plate lined with kitchen paper and keep warm while you fry the rest.

Serve the warm rice balls with the passion fruit dressing on the side.

Watermelon & Tomato Panzanella

SERVES 6–8

PICKLED WATERMELON

500g / 17½oz watermelon

2 cloves garlic, crushed

250ml / 1 cup cider vinegar

100ml / ⅓ cup sherry vinegar

50g / ¼ cup golden caster
   (superfine) sugar

75g / 6 tbsp light brown sugar

1 heaped tbsp sea salt flakes

SALAD

300g / 10½oz day-old
   sourdough bread

2 tbsp olive oil

3 cloves garlic, 1 whole, 2
   peeled and finely chopped

2 tbsp capers, chopped

2 tbsp chopped fresh flat leaf
   parsley

6 plum tomatoes, deseeded
   and finely chopped

4–6 ripe figs, chopped

1 red onion, finely sliced

½ cucumber, deseeded and
   cut into 2cm / ¾in cubes

100g / 1 cup Kalamata olives,
   pitted and chopped

small bunch of fresh basil,
   leaves roughly torn

salt and freshly ground
   black pepper

To make the pickled watermelon rind, cut the watermelon from the rind, cut the flesh into 5cm / 2in cubes, and set aside. Slice the rind into long thin strips and drop into a heatproof bowl with the crushed garlic.

Put the vinegars, sugars and salt into a pan and add 350ml / 1½ cups water. Bring to the boil, then pour over the watermelon rind in the bowl. Leave to cool.

Now make the salad. Drizzle the bread on both sides with some of the olive oil and toast on both sides in a frying pan. Rub each side of the toast with the whole garlic clove. Rip the garlic toast into 2.5cm / 1in cubes. Set aside.

Drain the cooled pickled watermelon rind and place in a large bowl. Add the toasted bread and all the remaining salad ingredients (including the watermelon flesh) and mix together. Season with salt and pepper.

Whisk all of the dressing ingredients together in a small bowl and pour over the salad. Toss together and leave to marinate in the refrigerator for 1 hour before serving.

DRESSING

3½ tbsp red wine vinegar

150ml / ⅔ cup extra virgin
   olive oil

1 clove garlic, crushed

pinch of sugar

Ackee & Fermented Black Beans / Walnut Dressing

SERVES 4

WALNUT DRESSING

2 tbsp each chopped fresh
  mint, parsley, dill and
  coriander (cilantro)
50g / 1/3 cup walnut halves,
  lightly toasted and
  crumbled
1 clove garlic, crushed
6 tbsp olive oil
2 tbsp lemon or lime juice
freshly ground black pepper

ACKEE & BEANS

2 tbsp Chinese fermented
  black beans, dried or
  canned
3 tbsp extra virgin olive oil
1 small red onion, very finely
  sliced
2 cloves garlic, crushed
6 sprigs of fresh thyme, leaves
  removed
1/2 Scotch bonnet chilli, finely
  chopped
4 spring onions (scallions),
  finely chopped
1/4 tsp ground allspice
540g / 20oz can of ackee,
  drained

This can be served on crisp little gem or round lettuce leaves with Rice & Peas underneath (see page 42). It also makes a quick and tasty starter, or can be tumbled onto small pieces of toasted bread.

Chinese fermented black beans are soft, salted black soya beans and can be found dried or in cans in Asian supermarkets.

Ackee is a tree-hanging fruit from the Caribbean that looks similar to a pomegranate. Once ripe, the fruit bursts open to reveal large black seeds (that are discarded) and pale yellow fleshy lobes which are eaten. You buy it canned, usually from the world food aisle of a supermarket.

First make the dressing in a small bowl by stirring the chopped herbs, walnuts, garlic and olive oil together, then add the lemon or lime juice and pepper to taste.

If using dried black beans, rinse them in cold water. If using canned beans, drain, then rinse. Chop the beans.

To cook the ackee, heat the olive oil in a large frying pan, add the red onion, garlic, thyme and chilli and cook over a medium heat for about 5 minutes or until softened. Add the spring onions (scallions), black beans and allspice, and cook for another minute or two. Now carefully stir in the ackee (it's very delicate) and heat for a few minutes until warmed through. Remove from the heat.

Drizzle some of the dressing over the ackee, and serve the rest on the side.

Rice & Peas

SERVES 6

200g / 1¼ cups dried kidney
  beans
2 cloves garlic, smashed
3 spring onions (scallions)
400ml / 13½fl oz coconut
  milk
¼ tsp ground allspice
400g / 2½ cups long-grain
  rice
2 sprigs of fresh thyme
1 Scotch Bonnet chilli
salt and freshly ground
  black pepper

QUICK VERSION

2 x 400g / 14oz cans kidney
  beans
1 x 400ml / 14fl oz can
  coconut milk
2 cloves garlic, smashed
2 spring onions (scallions)
1 Scotch bonnet chilli
1 sprig of fresh thyme
¼ tsp freshly ground
black pepper
350g / 2 cups long-grain rice,
  rinsed well and drained
salt

Put the kidney beans into a large bowl, pour over enough water to cover and leave to soak for at least 12 hours or overnight. Drain the beans, rinse well and drain again.

Tip the beans into a large saucepan and pour over 1 litre / 4½ cups of water. Add the garlic cloves, bring to the boil and boil for 10 minutes. Turn down the heat, cover and simmer for 45 minutes–1 hour or until just tender (it can take longer depending on the age of the beans).

Add the whole spring onions (scallions) to the pan with the beans and cook for another 30 minutes. Meanwhile rinse the rice well in cold water until the water runs clear. Stir the coconut milk and allspice into the beans, and then add the rice, the thyme and the whole chilli. Season, stir and bring to a simmer then cover tightly with foil and a lid. Turn the heat to low and cook for about 30 minutes without removing the lid, until tender.

Remove from the heat. Remove the garlic, spring onions, thyme and chilli. Fluff up the rice with a fork and season.

QUICK VERSION
Drain the liquid from the can of beans into a measuring jug and add the can of coconut milk, which should make about 700ml / 24fl oz liquid. Add enough water to top the liquid up to 1.2 litres / 40fl oz. Tip this liquid, the beans, garlic, spring onions (scallions), chilli and thyme into a large pan. Season with the pepper and salt to taste, bring to the boil, then stir in the rice. Bring back to the boil and simmer for 2 minutes.

Reduce the heat to low, and cook, covered tightly, for 15–20 minutes or until all the water is absorbed. Remove from the heat. Remove the garlic, spring onions, chilli and thyme. Fluff up the rice with a fork before serving.

Seeds of love

Chia, sunflower, pumpkin, hemp, sesame, brown linseed, flaxseeds, or the more unusual camelina – all these little seeds pack a good punch of protein and are highly nutritious. They're variably available as whole seeds, ground, hulled, ground into pastes or pressed as oils, so you can sprinkle on salads, use in breads and baking, whizz into energy balls and drizzle over toast.

Chia seeds, flaxseed and camelina seeds can each be used as an egg alternative.

Soak 1 tablespoon of seeds in 3 tablespoons of warm water for 30 minutes. This will replace one egg in baking. For another egg alternative, see aquafaba on page 70.

Any long-term vegan will tell you that choosing vegan means embarking on a journey. You might start by cutting back on certain foods, leaning on substitutes, or relaxing the rules a teeny, tiny bit when eating out or in a tricky situation. You might go on to living entirely vegan, avoiding all products (from leather to glue via beauty and fashion), that contain animal-derived products. How chilled or committed you are (or become) is your choice to make, and is something that will evolve and change. Be patient with yourself – and, to keep your friends, be patient with others!

Tomato Salad / Peanut Dressing

DRESSING

2 tbsp mirin

1 tbsp black rice vinegar

juice of 1½ limes

2 tsp golden caster
  (superfine) sugar

1 tbsp sesame oil

4 tbsp roasted, unsalted
  peanuts, crushed

1 red chilli, deseeded and
  finely chopped

4 cloves garlic, crushed

3 spring onions (scallions),
  finely chopped

¼ tsp salt

¼ tsp sugar

1 tsp sesame seeds

¼ tsp chilli powder

4 tbsp chopped fresh
  coriander (cilantro) leaves

2 tbsp chopped fresh basil
  leaves

3 tbsp chopped fresh mint
  leaves

SALAD

4 large ripe tomatoes

This peanut dressing (and the sesame dressing opposite) are very versatile. They are both great on any crunchy salad or dish with an Asian vibe.

Mix all of the ingredients for the dressing together in a bowl and set aside.

Using a sharp knife, cut the tomatoes into thick slices.

Lay the sliced tomatoes on a large serving plate and spoon over the peanut dressing.

Asparagus Soba Noodles / Sesame Dressing

SERVES 4 AS A STARTER OR SIDE DISH

NOODLES

250g / 9oz soba (buckwheat) noodles

1 tbsp sesame oil

500g / 17½oz asparagus spears, trimmed

6 spring onions (scallions), finely sliced

salt

DRESSING

5 tbsp mirin

5 tbsp light soy sauce

2.5cm /1in piece fresh root ginger, finely grated

wasabi paste, to taste

2 tbsp black sesame seeds

To cook the noodles, bring a large pan of lightly salted water to the boil and add the noodles, stirring to prevent them from sticking. Bring back to the boil, cooking the noodles for about 4–5 minutes or until just tender. Drain and refresh immediately in plenty of cold water. Drain well once more.

Place the drained noodles in a large bowl, add the sesame oil, toss well to combine and set aside.

Bring a pan of lightly salted water to the boil. Blanch the asparagus spears by dropping them into the boiling water for 2–4 minutes. Drain, and refresh the asparagus in a bowl of cold water, drain again and add to the bowl of noodles along with the sliced spring onions (scallions).

In a small bowl, mix together the mirin, soy sauce and ginger. Whisk in a little wasabi to taste then stir in the sesame seeds. Add enough of the dressing to the noodles to coat well and toss together.

Tofu Tikka / Beetroot Curry

‖‖

SERVES 4–6

TOFU TIKKA

2 tsp ground coriander

1 tsp ground cumin

½ tsp ground cloves

1 tsp paprika

1 tsp ground turmeric

2 tsp garam masala

finely grated zest and juice
of 1 lemon

1 red onion, roughly chopped

4 cloves garlic, crushed

5cm / 2in piece fresh root
ginger, roughly chopped

1–2 red chillies, deseeded and
finely chopped, or 1 tsp
dried chilli flakes

1 x 400g / 14oz can coconut
milk

1 tsp salt

1kg / 2¼lb firm tofu
(beancurd), cut into
2 x 4cm / ¾ x 1½in pieces

CURRY

4 tbsp vegetable oil

12 curry leaves (optional)

75g / 2⅔oz piece fresh root
ginger, peeled and finely
grated

4 cloves garlic, crushed

1 red chilli, deseeded and
finely chopped

6 green cardamom pods,
crushed

1 tsp ground cumin

1 cinnamon stick

finely grated zest and juice
of 1 orange

400g / 14oz can chopped
tomatoes

400ml / 14fl oz can coconut
milk

1 litre / 4½ cups vegetable
stock

8 raw beetroot (beets), with
leaves if possible, peeled
and cut into large chunks

1 tbsp palm or light brown
sugar, plus extra to taste

juice of 4 limes or 2 lemons,
or a mix of both

small bunch of fresh
coriander (cilantro),
chopped

salt and freshly ground
black pepper

TO SERVE

handful cashews, peanuts or
pecans, toasted and crushed

To make the marinade for the tofu (beancurd), put the ground coriander, cumin, cloves, paprika, turmeric and garam masala into a small dry pan and toast for 1 minute, then transfer to a large bowl.

Pour the lemon juice into a blender and add the zest, onion, ginger, garlic, chillies, coconut milk and salt, blend until smooth and pour into a bowl. Add the tofu pieces to the marinade and turn well to coat. Cover and leave to marinate in the fridge for a few hours, or overnight.

Meanwhile, to make the curry, heat the oil in a saucepan, add the curry leaves, if using, then add the garlic, ginger, chilli, cardamom, cumin, cinnamon and orange zest. Stir fry for about 3 minutes, then add the orange juice, tomatoes, coconut milk and stock. Season, bring to the boil, add the chopped beetroot (beets) and sugar, and bring to the boil again. Reduce the heat and simmer for 25–30 minutes, or until the beetroot is tender when tested with the point of a knife.

Meanwhile, wash the beetroot leaves, if using. Remove and discard any thick stalks, and chop the leaves roughly. Once the beetroot is tender, stir the leaves into the pot and cook until tender.

Preheat the oven to 220°C / 425°F/ gas mark 9.

Lift the tofu pieces from the marinade and lay them out on a baking tray (pan). Roast the tofu, for 20–25 minutes, basting with the remaining marinade occasionally, until lightly charred and heated through.

Check the curry for seasoning, and squeeze in half of the lime or lemon juice. Taste, adding more juice and sugar if desired, then stir in the chopped coriander (cilantro). Serve the curry topped with the tofu tikka and crushed nuts.

It's easy to live on a diet of carbs, but that's no life. Embrace vegan protein — beans, lentils, chickpeas, nuts and seeds, and, yes, tofu. Tofu is a sponge for spice and flavour. It's chicken's versatile soy cousin, so use it in curries, or batter and fry, as on the next page...

Salt & Pepper Tofu
/ Clementine & Chicory Salad

SERVES 4

SALT & PEPPER TOFU

1 block (300g / 10½oz)
   firm tofu (beancurd),
   drained well and dried
   on kitchen paper
zest of 1 clementine, finely
   grated
juice of 2 clementines
3cm / 1¼in piece fresh root
   ginger, finely grated
1–2 cloves garlic, very finely
   chopped
2 tbsp mirin
1 tbsp light soy sauce
1 tbsp sesame oil
sea salt and freshly ground
   black pepper
500ml / 2 cups vegetable
   or groundnut oil, for frying

SALAD
1 fennel bulb, very finely
   sliced
50g / ½ cup pitted black
   olives
seeds from ¼ pomegranate
2 clementines, peeled and
   sliced
1 head of chicory (endive),
   leaves pulled apart
½ radicchio, leaves pulled
   apart
4 radishes, finely sliced

BATTER
100g / ¾ cup self-raising
   (self-rising) flour, plus a
   little extra for dusting
100g / 1 cup cornflour
   (cornstarch)
1 tsp freshly ground
   white pepper
2 tsp sea salt
200ml / scant 1 cup
   sparkling water, chilled

First, marinate the tofu (beancurd). Cut the tofu into 3cm
/ 1¼in cubes and place in a bowl. Add the zest and juice
of the clementines, the ginger, garlic, a little salt and lots
of freshly ground black pepper.

Pour in the mirin, soy sauce and sesame oil and toss
together well. Cover and leave to marinate in the fridge
for an hour or preferably overnight, turning once. >>>

>>> Once marinated, drain the tofu well, reserving the marinade liquid.

Tip all the ingredients for the salad into a large bowl, add the reserved tofu marinade and toss well together.

Put a little flour onto a plate. Toss the tofu cubes in the flour.

To make the batter, mix together the flours, pepper and salt in a large bowl, then whisk in the sparkling water.

You can deep fry or shallow fry the tofu. To deep fry, heat the oil in a large, deep pan or wok. To check it is hot enough, drop a little of the mixture into the oil – it should turn golden brown in 40 seconds. (You can also shallow fry, if you wish: heat 150ml / ⅔ cup of oil in a deep frying pan and follow the method as above.)

Dip each of the tofu cubes into the batter and fry in batches in the hot oil until golden. Remove the cubes from the oil with a slotted spoon.

Drain on a plate lined with kitchen paper and serve the hot tofu on a bed of the salad.

Tasty toppings to try

///////////////////////

Herb Oils

Blanch the leaves of soft fresh herbs (such as basil or coriander) for a few seconds in boiling water. Then add to a blender (or use a stick blender). Drizzle in your oil of choice and blend to a smooth consistency. You can strain through a fine mesh sieve, if you like. Decant into a bowl or bottle and store in the fridge. Use over soups, salads and stews to lift dish to another level.

///////////////////////

Fried Breadcrumbs

Mollica is the Sicilian word for fried breadcrumbs – it's used to top pasta, salads, stews and even pizza – and it adds crunch and texture, which is ideal for vegan dishes. To make a stash, blitz stale bread in a food processor, then bag it up and freeze it. When you're ready to use, heat a little olive oil in a frying pan over a high heat, add the frozen breadcrumbs and fry until crispy.

Pizza Dough Base
/ Potato & Sage Topping

//////////////////////////////////

**MAKES TWO 23–25CM /
9–10IN THIN-CRUST
PIZZA BASES**

PIZZA DOUGH

250g / 1¾ cups strong white
bread flour, plus extra for
dusting

125g / 1 cup rye or semolina
flour

1 x 7g / ¼oz sachet easy-
bake yeast

2 tbsp olive oil, plus extra
for greasing

1 tsp sea salt

pinch of sugar

POTATO AND SAGE TOPPING

500g / 17½oz potatoes,
peeled and very thinly
sliced

2 tbsp extra virgin olive oil,
plus extra for drizzling

4 cloves garlic, crushed

2 sprigs of fresh sage, leaves
removed from the stalk

1½ tsp sea salt flakes

Sift the flours together into a large bowl and make a well
in the centre. Add the yeast, olive oil, sea salt and sugar
into the well. Measure 250ml / 1 cup warm water into
a jug (pitcher). Pour most of the warm water into the
bowl and mix everything together with a fork, then pull
together with your hands, adding more water if needed,
until a soft dough has formed.

Tip the dough out onto a lightly floured surface and knead
for 10 minutes until smooth and elastic. Place in a clean,
oiled bowl, cover and leave to rise at room temperature
for about an hour or until doubled in size.

Preheat the oven 220°C / 425°F / gas mark 9 and place
two large baking sheets in the oven to heat.

Place the potato slices, olive oil, garlic, sage and salt flakes
into a large bowl and toss together to coat.

Turn the pizza dough out onto a floured work surface, cut
into two pieces, and roll and pull each piece out to a large
circle about 23–25cm / 9–10in in diameter.

Remove the trays from the oven and carefully slide a pizza
base on to each one. Quickly spread the bases evenly with
the potato mixture. Drizzle with a little more olive oil and
bake for 15–20 minutes or until the potatoes are tender
and the pizza is lightly golden and crisp.

**You can make the pizza bases as above and spread
with sauce. Use ½ quantity Caponata (page 108). Don't
overload your bases, or they will get soggy.**

Panelle Fritters / Batons

**MAKES ABOUT 40 FRITTERS
OR BATONS TO SERVE 4–6**

2 x empty 400g / 14oz cans
vegetable oil, for frying and
  oiling the cans
300g / 2¼ cups chickpea
  (gram) flour
2 tbsp fresh rosemary leaves,
  chopped (optional)
salt and freshly ground
  black pepper
lemon wedges, to serve
soft bread rolls, to serve

**To make the batons,
make the mixture as
above but instead of
using the cans, pour the
hot mixture into a well-
oiled baking tray and
leave to set. Cut the
set mixture into chip-
like sticks.**

Oil the insides of the cans well with vegetable oil being careful of the sharp edges.

Sift the chickpea (gram) flour into a saucepan. Whisk in 750ml / 3¼ cups water slowly, working out any lumps. Stir in the chopped rosemary, if using, and salt and pepper to taste. Bring the mixture to the boil, beating all the time. Stir constantly until it is very thick. Don't worry if you get a few lumps – they will disappear when fried.

Scrape the mixture out of the pan and into the two cans. Tap them firmly on the table to remove any air bubbles and leave to cool and set for 1–2 hours at room temperature. If you are not cooking until later, then once cool, cover and place the cans in the fridge.

Once set, the panelle mixture should easily drop out of the cans, but if not – and to make slicing easier – use a can opener to open the other end of the can. Lay the can on its side and push the mixture through a little at a time, slicing thinly as you go, to make round fritters. Alternatively, remove from the can then cut the set mixture into rounds. You can cut again to make semicircle shapes.

Heat oil in a wok or deep fat fryer. The oil is ready when a piece of mixture sizzles instantly when dropped in. Deep fry a few fritters at a time, turning until golden brown. Drain on a plate lined with kitchen paper and sprinkle with salt. Use the same method for the batons (see left).

To oven bake, toss the fritters or batons lightly in a little oil and lay out on baking sheets in a single layer. Bake at 200°C / 400°F / gas mark 6 for 10–15 minutes for fritters, and 15–25 minutes for the batons, turning once or twice.

Serve hot with wedges of lemon and soft bread rolls.

Not everyone can keep up with today's ever more complex dietary choices — and since you don't want to crush Gran's spirit by turning down her creamy shepherd's pie (that you used to love!), make sure you plan ahead and communicate clearly. Call in advance and remind her of your fabulous new lifestyle. And then encourage her to feel a part of it. You could offer to arrive early and cook with her, so you can make a vegan option together. Or tell her you can bring a vegan dish for her to try. She may not be a convert, but at least there won't be tears in the mash.

Oven-baked Ratatouille

Preheat the oven to 190°C / 375°F / gas mark 5.

**SERVES 6 AS A MAIN DISH
OR 8 AS A SIDE DISH**

1kg / 2lb 4oz ripe tomatoes,
cores removed and roughly
chopped

2 onions, thickly chopped

few sprigs of fresh thyme

8 cloves garlic, peeled and
left whole

pinch of chilli flakes, optional

150ml / ⅔ cup extra virgin
olive oil

3 courgettes (zucchini), cut
into 3cm / 1¼in chunks

2 aubergines (eggplants), cut
into 3cm / 1¼in chunks

6 red peppers (bell peppers)
or a mixture or red and
yellow, cored and cut into
2.5cm / 1in strips

400g / 14oz can chickpeas
(garbanzo beans), drained
and rinsed

salt and freshly ground
black pepper

Put the chopped tomatoes, onions, thyme sprigs, garlic cloves and chilli flakes, if using, into a large roasting pan. Slosh over a few good glugs of the olive oil. Season well with salt and pepper, toss together, then place the tray into the top of the oven and roast for 45 minutes. Check on the vegetables every now then and give them a stir so that nothing burns.

Remove the pan from the oven and add the courgettes (zucchini). Return to the oven and continue to cook.

About 20 minutes later, add the aubergines (eggplants) and (bell) pepper strips to a second roasting pan and toss together well with salt, pepper and more of the olive oil.

Put the tray of aubergines and peppers below the tray of tomatoes, onions and courgettes in the oven and cook, turning occasionally, until nearly tender (about 30 minutes). Then add into the roasting tin with the tomatoes and stir. Add the chickpeas (garbanzo beans) and stir to mix once more.

Continue cooking the ratatouille for about another 20–30 minutes, until it looks totally gorgeous and squidgy. Check for seasoning and serve.

Falafel Patties / Cucumber Pickles / Nutty Dip

MAKES 8 PATTIES

FALAFEL PATTIES

250g / 1½ cups dried
   chickpeas (garbanzo beans)
½ red onion, finely chopped
2 cloves garlic, crushed
2 tbsp finely chopped fresh
   flat leaf parsley
2 tbsp finely chopped fresh
   coriander (cilantro)
½ tsp cayenne pepper
1 tsp ground cumin
1 tsp ground coriander
¼ tsp ground cinnamon
¼ tsp ground cardamom
¼ tsp ground nutmeg
½ tsp baking powder
1½ tbsp plain (all-purpose)
   flour or chickpea (gram)
   flour
4 tbsp sesame seeds
200ml / ¾ cup olive oil
salt and freshly ground
   black pepper

CUCUMBER PICKLES

350g / 12oz baby cucumbers
   or 1 large cucumber
2 tsp sea salt
½ tsp dried chilli flakes
   (optional)
300ml / 1¼ cups rice vinegar
½ tsp fennel seeds
2 tbsp golden caster
   (superfine) sugar
2 cloves garlic, crushed
1 tbsp black or white sesame
   seeds

NUTTY DIP

75g / 4 tbsp tahini (sesame
   paste)
50g / 3½ tbsp hazelnut butter
   or other nut butter
1–2 tbsp lemon juice
1 clove garlic, crushed
4 tbsp sesame seeds
salt

Place the chickpeas (garbanzo beans) in a large bowl, cover with water and set aside to soak overnight.

The next day, make the cucumber pickles. Cut small cucumbers into 1cm / ½in slices or a large cucumber into 4 x 1cm / 1½ x ½in batons and place them in a heatproof bowl or sterilized jar. >>>

>>> Add the rest of the ingredients for the pickles to a small pan. Bring to the boil and bubble for 1 minute, then remove from the heat. Pour the pickling liquid over the sliced cucumber, cover and set aside to cool.

To make the nutty dip, whisk all the ingredients and a pinch of salt together in a bowl. Add enough water to make a drizzling consistency. Set aside.

Make the falafel patties. Once soaked, drain and rinse the chickpeas and tip into the bowl of a food processor with the onion, garlic, parsley and coriander (cilantro). Pulse in batches, until finely chopped.

Scrape the mixture out into a bowl, add the spices, baking powder, flour, a pinch of salt and 3 tablespoons water and mix well to evenly combine. Cover and place in the fridge for an hour.

Remove the falafel mix from the fridge and, with wet hands, shape into 8 patties. Put the sesame seeds onto a plate, and gently roll the patties to coat them in sesame seeds, pressing down well.

Heat half the oil in a large frying pan and fry the patties, in batches, turning occasionally, until both sides are golden brown, adding more oil when needed.

Serve the patties warm with the cucumber pickles and the nut dip on the side.

Chickpeas are something of a vegan godsend. They are nutritious (a great source of manganese, iron and protein – all essential, obviously), affordable, widely available and very versatile.

Pop whole chickpeas into stews, blitz to make hummus, mould into falafel patties, bake (sprinkled with paprika) to create a crispy snack, and use as the 'meat' in tray bakes and curries. This wonder food generally adds umph, texture and body.

As well as the chickpeas themselves, you can make use of the drained liquid from the can (or the cooking liquid if you're using dried chickpeas) as a substitute for egg white – see the following page for more on the magical properties of aquafaba.

And then there's the pale yellow, powdery, gluten-free flour. Marketed as chickpea flour, gram flour or besan flour, it is effectively milled chickpeas. It has a rich, earthy flavour and can be used to help thicken sauces and soups, and as a binder in baking and flatbread-making. It's also ideal for making pancake batters, and coating fritters and vegetables before frying.

Use the aquafaba method below as a substitute in any recipes that call for egg whites. Master the art of aquafaba and you can also make merry with meringue and enjoy Eton mess, macarons and these cute whips (on the right) – see the full recipe on page 143.

Aquafaba

liquid drained from 1 x 400g / 14oz can of chickpeas (garbanzo beans)
½ tsp cream of tartar or lemon juice (optional)

Pour the water drained from the can of chickpeas (garbanzo beans) into a large bowl and use an electric hand-whisk or a stand mixer to whisk.

How long you whisk depends on how you're going to use the aquafaba. To use it as a binder or thickener, whisk for around 5 minutes until it has increased a little in volume and is white and foamy. The longer you whisk, the stiffer it will become. Approximately 10 minutes will give semi-stiff peaks, ideal for baking.

You can add the cream of tartar or lemon juice to help stabilise the mixture and result in stiffer peaks.

A rough guide

1 can chickpea liquid yields around 10 tablespoons of aquafaba

1 egg = 3 tablespoons aquafaba

1 egg white = 2 tablespoons aquafaba

Pisco Sour Lollies

**MAKES ABOUT 8 SMALL–
MEDIUM LOLLIES**

125g / ⅔ cup caster
  (superfine) sugar
100ml / 7 tbsp Pisco
100ml / 7 tbsp aquafaba – the
  drained water from a can of
  chickpeas (garbanzo beans)
100ml / 7 tbsp fresh lemon
  juice
75ml / 5 tbsp fresh lime juice
12 drops Angostura bitters

Put the sugar and 125ml / ½ cup water in a small pan over a low heat and stir until the sugar has dissolved. Remove from the heat, pour into a large bowl and leave to cool.

Once cool, add the Pisco, aquafaba, lemon juice, lime juice and Angostura bitters to the sugar syrup, mix and chill for 1 hour.

When chilled, whizz everything in a blender for about 1 minute, then half-fill 8 lolly moulds. Place the remaining lolly mix in the fridge. Freeze the moulds for about 1½ hours or until semi-frozen. Push a lolly stick upright in the centre of each lolly mould and return to the freezer for another 30 minutes or until frozen.

Once frozen whizz the remaining mixture in the blender again and top up the lollies to fill the moulds. Freeze for at least 4 hours or overnight, until completely solid.

Halva Cake / Peanut & Chickpea Praline

MAKES A 23CM / 9IN CAKE

2 x 400g / 14oz cans
  chickpeas (garbanzo beans)

200g / 7oz coconut oil

100g / ¾ cup unsalted, raw,
  skinned peanuts

200g / 1 cup golden caster
  (superfine) sugar

250g / 2 cups spelt flour,
  white or wholemeal

pinch of salt

2 tsp baking powder

2 tsp vanilla extract or paste

100g / 1 cup ground almonds
  or ground peanuts

200g / 7oz hulled hemp
  seeds

100g / 3½oz vegan halva,
  crumbled

vegan yoghurt, to serve
  (optional)

The praline in this recipe is very versatile. You could break it into pieces and serve as a petit four, grind it until fine to sprinkle on desserts, or blend into a smoothie.

Drain the chickpeas (garbanzo beans), reserving the water.

Line a 23 x 30cm / 9 x 12in baking sheet with parchment paper. Grease a 23cm / 9in round cake tin (pan) with a little of the coconut oil and line with parchment paper.

To make the praline, place the peanuts and 100g / ½ cup of the sugar in a small heavy-based pan. Heat gently until the sugar melts, swirling the pan frequently (rather than stirring, which can cause it to crystallize). Continue to cook, swirling occasionally, until the sugar turns a deep golden brown or reaches 165°C /330°F on a sugar thermometer.

Swirl in one-third of the drained chickpeas. Remove from the heat immediately and pour onto the lined baking sheet. Spread out in a single layer and leave to cool. When the praline has hardened (after about 30 minutes), break into small pieces.

Preheat the oven to 180°C / 360°F / gas mark 4.

To make the cake, sift the spelt flour, salt and baking powder into a large mixing bowl, tipping in any bits left in the sieve (strainer). >>>

>>> Whizz the remaining drained chickpeas in a food processor until very smooth, then scrape into another large bowl with a spatula.

Spoon the remaining coconut oil and vanilla into a small pan, place over a low-medium heat and heat until the oil has completely melted.

Whisk the melted oil and vanilla into the chickpea purée until smooth, then beat in the ground almonds, sieved flour mix and the hemp seeds.

Pour the reserved water from the drained chickpeas into a large bowl and use an electric hand-whisk or stand mixer to whisk for approximately 10 minutes until it has more than doubled in size and is white and foamy. Gradually add the remaining sugar and keep whisking until smooth and glossy.

Fold one-third of the meringue into the cake mixture, then carefully fold in the rest, along with the peanut and chickpea praline pieces. Pour the mixture into the prepared cake tin and sprinkle over the crumbled halva.

Bake for 1 hour 20–30 minutes, or until a skewer inserted into the middle of the cake comes out clean. Leave to cool a little before removing from the tin. Then transfer to a serving plate. Best served warm.

Snacks are key. Small treats you can carry around, keep at work in a box, hide at your mum's house or snaffle on the go: essential for plugging the 'everyone is eating but there's nothing for me' moments. See pages 4–5 and 12–13 for bars and balls.

Walnut & Potato Macaroons

MAKES ABOUT 30

MACAROONS

200g / 1½ cups walnut halves

75g / 2⅔oz cooked mashed
    potato*

finely grated zest of 1
    small lemon

200g / 1 cup golden caster
    (superfine) sugar

pinch of salt

COATING

150g / 1 cup walnut halves
    or a mix of 50g / ⅓ cup
    walnuts and 100g / ¾ cup
    sesame seeds

3 tbsp cornflour (cornstarch)

***If you don't have
leftover mash, bake a
potato in its skin in the
oven for 45 minutes
to 1 hour until tender
(a 100–150g / 3½–5oz
potato should be
enough to give you the
right quantity of mash,
but weigh at the end to
be sure). Leave to cool,
then peel and mash well
with a fork.**

**What? Potato in a macaroon? Yes! These are
gorgeous, little, gluten-free, sweet macaroons.
The potato gives them a good crunchy, yet chewy
texture. A great use for a little leftover mash.**

Preheat the oven to 180°C / 360°F / gas mark 4. Line
a couple of baking trays (pans) with parchment paper.

Whizz the walnuts up in a food processor until fine,
or crush in a plastic bag with a rolling pin.

Pour the crushed walnuts into a bowl and mix in the
mashed potato and lemon zest. Gradually blend in the
sugar and salt. Using a teaspoon, spoon the paste onto
a plate to make 30 even-sized pieces. Shape into balls.

Crush or finely chop the walnuts for the coating and
sprinkle on a large plate with the sesame seeds, if using.

Tip the cornflour (cornstarch) onto another plate and
pour some cold water into a small bowl. Roll each ball
of the macaroon mixture first in the cornflour, then in
the water, and finally in the walnuts and sesame seeds.

Place the coated balls on the baking trays leaving a little
space between them. Gently indent the top of each ball
with your finger. Bake for about 15–20 minutes, or until
the nuts are golden brown. Turn the trays around in the
oven once or twice to get an even colour.

Serve slightly warm or leave to cool and store for later.

Black Bean & Tahini Brownies

MAKES 16 BROWNIES

400g / 14oz can black (turtle) beans

100g / 3½oz Chinese fermented black beans, canned (drained weight), or substitute with more black beans

150g / ¾ cup black or white tahini (sesame paste)

200g / 7oz coconut oil

300g / 10½oz good-quality dark chocolate, 70% cocoa solids, broken into pieces

200g / 1 cup dark muscovado sugar

2 tsp vanilla extract or paste

200g / 1½ cups stoneground rye flour

250g / 1¼ cups golden caster (superfine) sugar

Black sesame paste is available in health food shops, but use white tahini if not available.

Drain the black (turtle) beans, reserving the water. Drain the fermented black beans, then rinse. Whizz the turtle beans with the fermented black beans and tahini paste in a blender or food processor until very smooth.

Preheat the oven to 180°C / 360°F / gas mark 4. Use a little of the coconut oil to grease and line a 26 x 21cm / 10½ x 8¼in or 20 x 25cm / 8 x 10in baking tin (pan) with parchment paper.

Place the remaining coconut oil in a large pan with 250g / 9oz of the chocolate, the muscovado sugar and the vanilla extract. Set over a medium-low heat, and stir occasionally until melted. Beat in the bean purée, then whisk in the rye flour. Set aside.

Pour the reserved water drained from the can of black beans into a large bowl and use an electric hand-whisk or stand mixer to whisk for approximately 10–15 minutes until it has more than doubled in size, and is pale grey and foamy. While still whisking, gradually add the golden caster (superfine) sugar until smooth and glossy.

Beat one-third of this meringue into the chocolate mixture, then gently fold in the rest. Pour the mixture into the lined baking tin and sprinkle evenly with the remaining chopped chocolate.

Bake for about 40 minutes, or until the surface of the brownie is starting to crack and is just set, but still wobbly in the centre. Remove from the oven and leave to cool in the tin before cutting into squares. Serve warm or cold.

Dry beans and chickpeas can be a faff, but they give a dish more texture and flavour than their canned counterparts. (Have canned to hand, though – they are great for throw-together meals.) Dried beans give roughly double the amount once soaked, cooked and drained. This varies from bean to bean, but it's a decent guide.

Be an ambassador for vegan living.

Delivering a positive message about the benefits of being vegan — for people, planet and animal welfare — will have a greater impact than expressing frustration, defensiveness or anger. For those who ask (sometimes annoying) questions, find the patience to give the answers and you will be helping to educate and inform. And who knows, those naysayers may well change. Equally, nurture your own curiosity and seek your own answers — it will better equip you to move forward on your journey of vegan discovery.

Seedy Seaweed Crackers

15g / ½oz dried seaweed (sea
lettuce, bladderwrack,
hijiki, arame or wakame),
finely chopped
100g / ¾ cup wholemeal
spelt flour
150g / 1 heaped cup
white spelt flour
1 tsp fine salt
25g / 2 tbsp coconut oil, plus
a little extra for greasing
50g / ⅓ cup ground
flaxseeds
1 tbsp black or white
sesame seeds
¼ tsp chilli powder or
chilli flakes
1 tsp sugar
150ml / ⅔ cup almond or
other nut milk
sea salt flakes
Broad Bean Dip (page 86),
to serve

Preheat the oven to 200°C / 400°F / gas mark 6. Lightly grease four 20 x 30cm / 8 x 12in baking sheets with a little coconut oil.

Put the dried seaweed in a bowl and pour over enough boiling water to cover. Leave for 30 minutes, then drain and very finely chop.

Sift the flours and salt into a large bowl. Add the coconut oil and rub into the flour with your fingertips until it resembles fine breadcrumbs.

Stir in the ground flaxseeds, sesame seeds, chilli, sugar, and chopped seaweed. Slowly add the milk and bring the mixture together until it forms a soft but firm dough.

Divide the dough into four pieces and roll out each piece to a large rectangle about 20 x 30cm / 8 x 12in. Trim the edges and transfer each piece to a prepared baking sheet.

Score the surface into 5cm / 2in squares with a knife. Sprinkle with sea salt flakes and bake for 8–10 minutes until lightly golden.

Remove from the oven and carefully turn the pieces of dough over. Return to the oven for a further 5–6 minutes.

Remove from the oven and cool on a wire rack. Break the crackers apart.

To enjoy, dip into the dip (on the following page)!

Broad Bean Dip
/ Spiced Onions

SERVES 8

BEAN DIP

225g / 1¼ cups dried, split
  broad (fava) beans
4 tbsp extra virgin olive oil,
  plus extra to drizzle
1 onion, finely chopped
1 carrot, finely chopped
1 stick celery, finely
  chopped
2 cloves garlic, crushed
sea salt and freshly ground
  black pepper

SPICED ONIONS

3 tbsp extra virgin olive oil
3 onions, thinly sliced
  into rings
½ tsp ground cinnamon
¼ tsp ground allspice
pinch of chilli flakes

**To simplify this dip, use
canned beans, adding
them to the cooked veg
before blitzing. You can
also use the dip as a
purée to top crostini, or
as a sandwich spread for
added protein.**

Soak the beans overnight in enough water to cover them.

The next day, drain, rinse and tip the beans into a large
pan. Pour over enough water to cover and bring to the
boil. Skim off any scum that rises to the surface, reduce
the heat and simmer for about 1½ hours, or until the
beans are tender. Once cooked, drain the beans, reserving
the cooking liquid.

While the beans are cooking, make the spiced onions.
Heat the olive oil in a large pan, add the sliced onions and
cook over a medium heat for about 15 minutes, stirring
occasionally, until very soft and caramelized. Stir in the
spices, season, and cook for 2 minutes more. Transfer the
onions to a plate and set aside.

Once the beans have cooked, heat 3 tablespoons of
the olive oil in a pan over a medium-low heat. Add the
chopped onion, carrot, celery and garlic and cook for
5–8 minutes until soft.

Put the cooked beans and vegetables into the bowl of
a food processor (you may need to do this in batches).
Whizz until smooth with a ladleful of the reserved bean
cooking liquid and the remaining tablespoon of olive
oil, adding more liquid if needed to make a smooth but
thick purée.

Scrape out into a bowl and season to taste. Serve warm or
at room temperature, sprinkled with the fried onions and
drizzled with a little more olive oil.

Chipotle Cashews

SERVES 6

300g / 2½ cups cashews
2 tsp chipotle in adobo sauce,
   chopped
1 tsp fennel seeds
pinch of ground cinnamon
3 tbsp currants
1 tbsp dark brown sugar
1 tbsp apple cider vinegar
1 tbsp sesame seeds
freshly ground black pepper
sea salt flakes

Preheat the oven to 150°C / 300°F / gas mark 2. Line a baking tray (pan) with parchment paper.

Mix all the ingredients, except the salt, together in a bowl, until everything is nicely coated. Spread the mixture out evenly on the lined tray.

Place the tray in the oven and roast for 10 minutes. Remove from the oven, toss the nuts, then return to the oven for another 5–10 minutes or until golden.

Remove from the oven, sprinkle with sea salt flakes, toss together once more and leave to cool.

Serve or keep in an airtight container for about a week.

Fennel-roasted Chickpeas

SERVES 6

400g / 14oz can chickpeas
   (garbanzo beans), drained
   and rinsed
2 tbsp olive oil
finely grated zest and juice
   of ½ lemon
2 cloves garlic, crushed
1 tsp ground cumin
1 tsp ground coriander
1 tsp fennel seeds, crushed
1 tsp smoked paprika
1 tsp sea salt flakes

Preheat the oven to 200°C / 400°F / gas mark 6.

Mix all the ingredients together in a bowl and spread out evenly on a baking tray (pan).

Roast in the oven for 30–35 minutes, stirring once or twice during cooking, until the chickpeas are golden and crunchy.

Serve or keep in an airtight container for about a week.

Salted Turmeric Peanuts

300g / 2¼ cups raw, unsalted
  peanuts
3 tbsp currants
1 clove garlic, crushed
3cm / 1in piece fresh root
  ginger, finely grated
1 tbsp unsweetened
  desiccated (dried shredded)
  coconut
½ tsp ground turmeric
1 tbsp coconut oil, melted
½ tsp chilli powder
sea salt flakes

Preheat the oven to 150°C / 300°F / gas mark 2. Line a baking tray (pan) with parchment paper.

Mix all the ingredients, except the salt, together in a bowl and spread out evenly on the lined tray.

Place the tray in the oven and roast for 10 minutes. Toss the nuts and return to the oven for another 5 minutes or until golden.

Remove from the oven, sprinkle with sea salt flakes, toss together once more and leave to cool.

Serve or keep in an airtight container for about a week.

Rice Paper Rolls
/ Pickled Ginger & Radishes

MAKES 20

PICKLES

200g / 7oz fresh root ginger

1½ tsp sea salt

300g / 10½oz radishes,
trimmed and sliced in half

2 cloves garlic, finely sliced

200ml / ¾ cup rice vinegar

2 heaped tbsp caster
(superfine) sugar

RICE PAPER ROLLS

½ quantity Sushi Rice
(page 97)

25g / 1oz sea lettuce or other
dried seaweed like wakame,
arame or hijiki (optional)

20 dried rice paper discs
(20cm / 8in)

marigold petals or other
edible flower petals
(optional)

2 raw beetroot, peeled and
cut into fine matchsticks

2 large carrots, peeled and
cut into fine matchsticks

light soy sauce, to serve

Make the pickles a day in advance, if possible, or at least a few hours before serving. They will keep for 3–4 weeks in the fridge.

To make the pickles, peel the ginger, then slice into ribbons with a vegetable peeler. Bring a small pan of water to the boil. Place the ginger ribbons in a small bowl, sprinkle with ½ teaspoon of the salt and allow to sit for 5 minutes, then blanch in the boiling water for 3 minutes.

Drain well and squeeze the water out of the ginger with your hand. Drop the ginger into a sterilized jar with the radish halves and garlic slices.

Pour 300ml / 1¼ cups water, the rice vinegar, sugar and remaining salt into a small pan, and place over a medium heat, stirring to dissolve the sugar. Raise the heat, bring to the boil and bubble for a couple minutes, then pour the liquid over the vegetables in the jar. Leave to cool, before refrigerating until ready to serve.

Make the Sushi Rice (page 97), leave to cool slightly, then cover and place in the fridge until completely cold.

Meanwhile, if using dried seaweed, put it into a bowl, cover with cold water and leave to soak for 30 minutes, or until softened, then drain.

To make the rolls, prepare a large bowl of cold water and have all the ingredients ready in front of you on a clean work surface. >>>

>>> Working with one at a time, submerge the rice papers into the bowl of water for about a minute or until completely softened. Lift the softened paper out of the water, shaking off any excess, and lay flat on the work surface.

Working about one-third the way up the paper, sprinkle on a few petals, if using, a few vegetable strips and a little seaweed, if using, to make a line horizontally across the rice paper. Scoop a large tablespoon of the rice mixture and arrange it in a line along the top of the vegetables.

Fold over the edge of the rice paper closest to you to cover the filling, and half roll up. Fold in the edges on either side and roll up completely. Put the completed roll onto a tray and keep refrigerated. Repeat with the remaining ingredients.

Serve the rolls with the pickled vegetables and soy sauce for dipping.

A balanced and nutritious diet results in a happy, healthy vegan.

Eat bright, fresh, seasonal and varied food and it's unlikely you'll have a problem. But it's good to be mindful of your intake of certain vitamins and minerals, particularly if you're newly giving up meat, fish or dairy. Look after your bones by considering your calcium levels. Go for a calcium triple whammy by making a stir fry with pak choi, edamame beans and tofu; double up by snacking on dried figs and almonds; or simply top up your calcium with a side of kale or spring greens. And think about your essential fats. Aim for a balance of omega-3 and omega-6 fats by eating chia seeds, hemp seeds and walnuts, as well as pumpkin and sunflower seeds. Keep your immune system strong with good levels of iron (broccoli, spinach and tofu) and iodine (cranberries, strawberries and seaweed). Zinc and vitamin B_{12} are more complicated as the main source is red meat. For zinc, look to oats, tofu, cashews, chickpeas and lentils. B_{12} (essential for the nervous system) can't be found in plants. You can score a bit in that ever-divisive product, Marmite, as well as other foods fortified with B_{12}. But do consider a supplement to get your recommended daily allowance. Of course, a good multi-vitamin goes a long way when it comes to all these vitamins and minerals. It's your call.

Mushroom & Seaweed Caviar

SERVES 8–10 AS A DIP

5g / ¼oz dried mixed wild
  mushrooms
10g / ⅓oz dried seaweed
  (sea lettuce, bladderwrack,
  hijiki, arame or wakame)
500g / 17½oz mixed field
  mushrooms or chestnut
  (cremini) mushrooms
3 tbsp olive oil
6 spring onions (scallions),
  finely sliced
2 cloves garlic, crushed
50g / ½ cup pitted black
  olives, finely chopped
10g / ½ cup fresh dill,
  chopped, plus extra
  for serving
juice of 1 lemon
pinch of paprika
¼ nutmeg, finely grated,
  or ¼ teaspoon ground
  nutmeg
salt and freshly ground
  black pepper

Dark and luxuriously rich, this is perfect to feed a crowd as a dip with crackers (or to top little pancakes, such as the Buckwheat Dosa Blini on page 97). It's also wonderful stirred into soups and broths just before serving.

Place the dried mushrooms and seaweed in a bowl and pour over enough boiling water to cover. Leave to soak for 30 minutes, then drain and finely chop.

Break the fresh mushrooms into rough pieces directly into the bowl of a food processor, then whizz until finely chopped (you'll need to do this in batches).

Heat the oil in a large frying pan, add the spring onions (scallions) and garlic and cook for about 2 minutes or until softened. Add the chopped fresh mushrooms and the dried, soaked, chopped mushrooms and seaweed and cook over a moderate heat. Water will start to come out of the mushrooms – carry on cooking until all the liquid has evaporated, stirring frequently, for about 15–20 minutes or until the mushrooms are dark and rich in colour. Set aside to cool.

Stir the olives and dill into the cooled mushroom mixture, add the lemon juice, paprika and nutmeg, and season to taste with salt and pepper. (You may not need too much salt as the olives will be quite salty.)

Serve with an extra sprinkle of chopped dill.

Vegan sushi filling options are many and varied: stuff with your choice of avocado, mango, mushroom, cucumber, carrot, chestnuts, spring onions, tofu... then add chilli, roll in sesame seeds, wrap in nori seaweed sheets or top with fresh herbs.

Buckwheat Dosa Blini

**MAKES ABOUT 50 LITTLE
CANAPÉ-SIZED PANCAKES**
100g / ¾ cup rice flour
50g / 3½ tbsp buckwheat
   flour
½ tsp salt
vegetable oil, for frying

Add the two flours to a large bowl with the salt. Whisk in enough water to make a thin batter.

Set a non-stick frying pan over a medium-hot heat and brush with oil. Use a tablespoon to drizzle a spoonful of the batter back and forth in swirly patterns, filling the centres (photo on page 95). Each blini should be about 7 x 4cm / 2¾ x 1½ in.

Cook the blini for a few minutes, turning once, until both sides are lightly golden. Remove from pan and keep warm while you continue to cook the rest of the batter.

Sushi Rice

SERVES 4
450g / 2¼ cups sushi rice
1 piece dried kombu or
   kelp seaweed
4 tbsp rice vinegar
2 tbsp caster (superfine)
   sugar
1 tsp fine salt

Put the rice in a pan with the kombu or kelp, and add 630ml / 2⅔ cups boiling water. Cover tightly and simmer over a medium heat for 18–20 minutes until tender.

Remove from the heat. Allow to stand for 5 minutes, then stir in the vinegar, sugar and salt.

Use to make sushi, sushi rolls, as a filling for Rice Paper Rolls (see page 90), or for Ginger Tofu Rice Balls (see page 36).

Keeps for 3–4 days in the fridge.

Pisco Sour

SERVES 2

100ml / 7tbsp Pisco

100ml / 7tbsp aquafaba –
drained water from a can of
chickpeas (garbanzo beans)

50ml / 3½ tbsp lime or lemon
juice

2 tsp caster (superfine) sugar

ice cubes

a few drops Angostura bitters

Shake everything except the bitters in a cocktail shaker
without ice for 20–30 seconds. Add the ice and shake
again for a further 20–30 seconds.

Pour into two glasses and splash in a few drops of
Angostura bitters.

Padrón Pea Pods

SERVES 2–3

300g / 10½oz young peas
in the pods

6 tbsp extra virgin olive oil

sea salt flakes

pul biber (Aleppo pepper)
or other chilli flakes

**This is based on the
Galician dish using
Padrón peppers. Eat the
whole pods if tender or
pull out the peas with
your teeth as you might
do with edamame pods.**

Heat a large frying pan over a medium-high heat. Working
in batches, add 2 tablespoons of the oil and a handful of
pea pods to the pan and stir fry, tossing frequently.

When the first batch is nearly tender, after 1–2 minutes,
add a pinch of sea salt and chilli flakes and toss again,
cooking for 1–2 minutes longer until the pods are tender.

Tip the cooked pods onto a tray and repeat with the rest
of the pea pods.

Perfect served with an ice-cold beer or cocktail like the
Pisco Sour, above.

Potato & Squash Gnocchi / Pesto Trapanese

SERVES 6–8

GNOCCHI

750g / 1lb 10½oz large
  potatoes
500g / 17½oz butternut
  squash, peeled, deseeded
  and cut into 4cm / 1½in
  cubes (350g / 12oz trimmed
  weight)
2 tbsp olive oil
125g / 1 cup plain
  (all-purpose) flour, plus
  extra for rolling

PESTO TRAPANESE

3 ripe tomatoes, roughly
  chopped
4 cloves garlic, roughly
  chopped
50g / 2 cups fresh basil leaves,
  chopped
125g / 1 cup blanched
  almonds, toasted or
  untoasted
150ml / ⅔ cup extra virgin
  olive oil
salt and freshly ground
  black pepper

You can freeze the gnocchi: make and shape the dough, lay it in a single layer on a tray and freeze until solid, then drop the frozen gnocchi into freezer bags to store. Cook directly from frozen – they are ready as soon as they rise to the surface of the boiling water.

Preheat the oven to 200°C / 400°F / gas mark 6.

First, make the pesto. Place all the ingredients in a food processor and blend until finely chopped. Alternatively, finely chop all the ingredients by hand, and stir everything together to give a chunky sauce. Season and set aside.

To make the gnocchi, prick the potatoes two or three times with a fork and bake in oven for about 45 minutes to 1 hour, or until tender.

Place the butternut squash cubes on a baking tray, add the olive oil and a pinch of salt and toss well. Add to the oven and roast for 30–40 minutes or until very tender.

When the potatoes are cool enough to handle, but still warm, peel off the skins, drop into a large bowl and mash well until smooth. Add the cooked squash to the bowl with the potato and mash well once more.

Beat in the flour, a little at a time. Stop adding flour when the mixture is smooth and slightly sticky. Season with salt.

Turn the mixture out onto a floured board and roll out into cylinders about about 34cm / 13½in long, with a 2cm / ¾in diameter. Cut each roll into 3cm / 1¼in lengths. >>>

>>> Taking one piece at a time, press the gnocchi onto a floured fork. Roll each piece slightly while pressing it along the prongs and flip it off the fork onto a floured plate or tray (as you do this you will create a little dimple in the centre of each gnocchi that ensures they cook evenly). Continue with the rest of the gnocchi.

Bring a large pan of water to the boil and drop in 20–25 pieces of gnocchi at a time. They will rise to the surface very quickly. Let them cook for 10–15 seconds more. Lift them out with a slotted spoon and keep them warm while you continue with the remaining gnocchi.

To serve, toss the hot gnocchi with the pesto.

Try not to obsess over substitutions and replacements for classic meat or dairy dishes. Instead, aim to shift the way you think about food, how you eat and how you shop. Be open and adventurous in both the supermarket and the kitchen; consider previously unexplored wholefoods and vegetables. Be bold and a whole world of food will open to you.

Seek global inspiration for 'accidentally' vegan dishes — explore Vietnamese, Thai, Japanese and Middle Eastern cuisine for vibrant ideas.

Mole Poblano
/ Green Apple Salsa

SERVES 6

4 dried Ancho chillies

2 dried Mulato chillies

2 dried Pasilla chillies
(or replace all of the above
with 3–4 tsp chilli flakes)

500g / 17½oz pumpkin or
butternut squash, peeled,
deseeded, and cut into
4cm / 1½in cubes

3 aubergines (eggplants), cut
into 4cm / 1½in cubes

2 onions, roughly chopped

6 cloves garlic, skin on

120ml / ½ cup olive oil

½ tsp ground cinnamon

1 tsp fennel (or anise) seeds

10 black peppercorns

6 allspice berries

½ tsp coriander seeds

½ tsp cloves

1 tsp dried oregano

5 tbsp vegetable oil

2 tbsp raisins

50g / 6 tbsp cacao nibs,
or 100g / 3½oz dark
chocolate, chopped

100g / ¾ cup whole blanched
almonds

50g / ⅓ cup raw, whole
unsalted peanuts

50g / 6 tbsp pumpkin seeds

50g / 6 tbsp sesame seeds

2 stale tortillas, or 2 slices
day-old bread (about 50g
/ 1¾oz), torn into pieces

1 litre / 4½ cups vegetable
stock

400g / 14oz can chopped
tomatoes

2 tbsp dark brown sugar or
date syrup

salt and freshly ground black
pepper

APPLE SALSA

1 small onion, chopped

1 Jalapeño or other green
chilli, deseeded and
chopped

½ small cucumber, finely
chopped

handful of coriander
(cilantro) stalks,
chopped, plus 2 tbsp
chopped leaves

juice of 1–2 limes

½ green apple, finely
chopped

pinch of caster (superfine)
sugar

TO SERVE

corn tortillas, warmed

The traditional trinity
of chillies for Mole
Poblano consists of
Ancho, Mulato and
Pasilla. But you can
mix and match your
own choice of Mexican
chillies, balancing
hot, sweet and smoky
flavours. Most major
supermarkets stock
a good range of whole
and ground Mexican
chillies, or find a good
range online.

If using whole chillies, destem, deseed (if you like) and tear the chillies into large flat pieces. Place in a dry frying pan over a medium-high heat and dry roast for a few minutes, but don't let them burn.

Once toasted, put the chillies into a bowl, add enough warm water just to cover and leave to soften for 1 hour.

If using chilli flakes, no need to soak. Simply toast on a low heat. (If you toast on a high heat, they will burn and fill your kitchen with a fiery smoke!)

Preheat the oven to 200°C / 400°F / gas mark 6.

Put the pumpkin or squash, aubergines (eggplants), onions and whole garlic cloves into a large roasting pan. Pour over the olive oil, sprinkle with a little salt and toss well to coat. Roast the vegetables for 30–40 minutes, or until tender. Remove from the oven and set aside.

Remove the garlic cloves from the pan and when cool enough to handle, squeeze out the garlic flesh into the bowl of a blender or food processor.

Add the mole spices and herbs to a dry pan over a low-medium heat and cook for 2–3 minutes, turning frequently. Tip the toasted spices and herbs into the blender bowl with the garlic.

Add 2 tablespoons of the vegetable oil to the pan, add the raisins and cacao nibs (if you're using chocolate, don't add at this stage). Cook until the raisins plump up. Scoop out of the oil with a slotted spoon, and into the blender bowl.

Add the almonds and peanuts to the pan and toast until golden. Add this to the blender bowl. >>>

>>> Add another tablespoon of oil to the pan and add the pumpkin and sesame seeds, toasting until lightly golden. Once again, scoop them out into the blender bowl.

Finally, add the tortilla or bread pieces to the pan and toast until crisp and golden. Add to the blender bowl along with the chillies and their soaking water and whizz everything together until you have a fine paste.

Heat the remaining 2 tablespoons vegetable oil in a large pan, scrape the paste into the pan and cook gently for 5 minutes on a low heat (be careful not to burn it). Pour in the vegetable stock, chopped tomatoes and the sugar or syrup, stir, and cook for 45 minutes, stirring frequently and being careful that the sauce doesn't catch on the base of the pan and burn.

Stir in the roasted pumpkin, aubergines and onions. If you're using chopped chocolate (rather than nibs), add this too. Cook for a further 30 minutes.

To make the salsa, drop the chopped onion, chilli, half of the cucumber, the coriander (cilantro) stalks, juice of 1 of the limes and 1 tablespoon of water into the bowl of a food processor. Pulse until you have a rough salsa.

Scrape out into a bowl, stir in the remaining cucumber, the apple and the coriander leaves. Add the sugar and season with salt and pepper to taste, adding more lime juice if you like.

Serve the mole with warm corn tortillas and the salsa.

Caponata

SERVES 4–6

4 tbsp extra virgin olive oil

1 large onion, chopped

1 celery stick, sliced into
2cm / ¾in pieces

400g / 14oz really ripe large
tomatoes, roughly chopped
(or a 400g / 14oz can of
chopped tomatoes)

1 large aubergine (eggplant)
(about 400g / 14oz), cut
into 4cm / 1½in cubes

vegetable oil, for deep frying

1 tbsp capers, rinsed well in
warm water, drained and
chopped

50g / ½ cup pitted green
olives

1–2 tbsp red wine vinegar

1–1½ tbsp caster (superfine)
sugar

handful of fresh flat leaf
parsley, chopped

sea salt and freshly ground
black pepper

An unctuous, Sicilian sweet and sour aubergine stew that can be served cold as an antipasto or warm as a vegetable main, starter or side.

Heat the olive oil in a saucepan and add the chopped onion and celery. Cook for 5–6 minutes until softened. Add the chopped tomatoes and cook for 15 minutes until pulpy.

Meanwhile, heat the vegetable oil in a large deep pan. When a piece of aubergine (eggplant) is dropped in, it should bubble immediately. Deep fry the aubergine, in batches, turning occasionally, until the pieces are golden brown and very soft. Scoop out the cooked aubergine pieces with a slotted spoon. Drain on a tray lined with kitchen paper.

Once the tomatoes are pulpy, add the chopped capers and olives. Season, add 1 tablespoon of vinegar and 1 tablespoon of sugar and continue cooking for another 15–20 minutes or until you have a thick gloopy sauce.

Stir the cooked aubergines into the tomato sauce, and simmer for another 10 minutes. Taste and adjust the seasoning, adding more vinegar and sugar as needed to get a good sweet and sour flavour.

Stir the chopped parsley into the stew and leave to stand for at least an hour before serving to allow the flavours to develop.

Water Chestnut Gyoza

//

MAKES ABOUT 36 DUMPLINGS

DUMPLING DOUGH

300g / 2¼ cups plain
  (all-purpose) flour
  or dumpling flour

FILLING

150g / 5oz Chinese cabbage
  leaves, finely chopped
1 tbsp sesame oil
2 tbsp vegetable oil, plus
  extra for frying the gyoza
2 large shallots, finely
  chopped

3 cloves garlic, crushed
5cm / 2in piece fresh root
  ginger, finely grated
½ tsp ground cinnamon
1 tbsp Shaoxing rice wine
8 canned water chestnuts,
  drained and finely chopped
salt and freshly ground
  black pepper

DIPPING SAUCE

3 tbsp soy sauce
2 tbsp mirin
2 tbsp white miso paste
2 tbsp rice vinegar
2 tbsp sesame oil

Making your own dumpling wrappers is easy and uses only flour and water. For a finer dough, buy dumpling flour, available from Asian supermarkets. Alternatively, you can use store-bought dumpling wrappers.

To make the dough, tip the flour onto a clean work surface, make a well in the centre and pour in 180ml / ¾ cup cold water. Quickly bring together with your fingers to make a stiff but pliable dough. Knead the dough for about 10 minutes, or until smooth and elastic. Cover the dough on the work surface with a bowl and leave to rest for 30 minutes.

To make the filling, place the chopped Chinese cabbage leaves in a colander, sprinkle with a little salt and toss together well. Set aside for 10 minutes, then rinse and dry well. >>>

>>> Heat the oils for the filling in a frying pan over a low-medium heat. Add the chopped shallots, garlic and ginger and cook for 5 minutes or until softened. Add the cinnamon and cook for 30 seconds, then add the chopped cabbage. Raise the heat, add the rice wine and stir fry for a minute more until softened. Remove from the heat and stir in the water chestnuts. Transfer the filling mix to a bowl, season and leave to cool.

To make the dipping sauce, whisk all the ingredients together in a small bowl.

To make the dumplings, divide the dough into four pieces and roll out each piece into a 18cm / 7in cylinder of around 2–2.5cm / ¾–1in diameter. Cut each of the cylinders into nine 2cm / ¾in rounds.

Place each round of dough on a floured board and flatten with the palm of your hand. With a rolling pin, roll each piece into a 7cm / 2¾in disc, rolling into the centre and turning all the time. This way the edges of the circles will be thinner than the centre.

Lay the dumpling wrappers on a tray, dusting lightly in between each one if stacking them up.

Fill a small bowl with cold water. Taking one dumpling wrapper at a time in the cup of your hand, place a heaped teaspoon of the cooled filling mixture into the middle. Dip a finger into the bowl of water and brush round the inside edge of the wrapper, then carefully fold both sides up over the filling, pinching from one end to the other to seal along the top. Repeat with the remaining wrappers and filling.

To cook the dumplings, heat a large frying pan (that has a lid) over a medium-hot heat and add a tablespoon of the vegetable oil. In batches, add the dumplings to the pan, base side down, and cook for 2–3 minutes or until golden on the bottom. Then raise the heat, pour in a small cup of water and cover with the lid. Cook for 2 minutes more, until the water has evaporated and the dumplings are tender and heated through.

Keep the cooked dumplings warm while you repeat with the remaining dumplings, adding more oil if needed.

Serve the dumplings with the dipping sauce.

A good store cupboard can be a saviour, so be generous and experimental.

Stock with grains (barley, rye, spelt, teff), lentils (Puy, red, brown, yellow, green), beans (black, aduki, cannellini, lima), and all the nuts and seeds. Think about a jar of tahini and/or miso paste too. Tahini is rich in B vitamins and essential fats, while miso is great for gut health. Both form ideal dressing bases.

Making vegetable stock is a variable process, depending on what you have in the fridge. This is not a strict ingredient list, but it does create a brilliant stock. Adapt with the herbs, spices and vegetables you like. The tomatoes give a rich flavour, but don't add them if you want a more delicate stock.

Vegetable stock

MAKES ABOUT 2 LITRES / 3½ PINTS

2 leeks
6 carrots
3 celery sticks
3 onions
1 fennel bulb
1 whole head garlic, cut in half horizontally
1 tsp black peppercorns
1 lemon, cut into wedges
6 bay leaves
2 star anise, optional
1 large sprig thyme
small handful of parsley stalks
6 ripe tomatoes, roughly chopped (optional)

Roughly chop all of the vegetables. Place them in a large, deep pan with all the remaining ingredients. Cover with 3 litres / 6½ cups cold water and set over a high heat.

Bring to a boil, then reduce the heat to low and simmer for 30 minutes.

Remove from the heat and leave to cool completely, which will help the flavours to infuse.

Strain through a fine sieve (strainer) and store in the fridge. It will keep for 5–6 days. You can also freeze it in small containers or bags, so you always have a great stock at hand.

Wild Mushroom Pierogi

**MAKES ABOUT 25–30
DUMPLINGS**

FILLING

4 large floury potatoes, about
    1kg / 2lb 3oz
3 tbsp vegetable or
    sunflower oil
2 onions, very finely chopped
    salt and freshly ground
    black pepper

DOUGH

450g / 3½ cups plain
    (all-purpose) flour, plus
    extra for dusting
1 tsp fine salt
1 tbsp vegetable or
    sunflower oil

TO SERVE

100ml / 7 tbsp olive oil
350g / 12oz mixed wild and
    cultivated mushrooms,
    sliced if large
3 tbsp chopped fresh
    flat leaf parsley
juice of 1 lemon

To make the filling, peel and quarter the potatoes. Bring a pan of water to the boil and cook the potatoes until tender, then drain and mash well.

Heat the oil in a frying pan, add the chopped onions and fry until softened and golden. Add the onion to the bowl with the mash. Stir to combine, and season to taste.

To make the dough, tip the flour into a large bowl with the salt and the oil. Fill a measuring jug with 125ml / ½ cup of lukewarm water. Gradually add enough of the water to make a soft dough, using a fork at first, then using the tips of your fingers to bring it together.

Tip the dough out onto a clean, lightly floured work surface. Knead well for about 5 minutes or until smooth. Dust the surface with a little extra flour every now and then so it doesn't stick.

Roll out the dough to about 3mm / ⅛in thick. Using a 7cm / 2¾in pastry cutter, cut out 25–30 rounds.

Fill a pan with water and bring to the boil.

Taking one round of dough in your hand at a time, add a tablespoon of the filling to the centre and bring the two edges of the dough together. Pinch to seal, then flute the edges from one end to the other. Continue with the remaining dough and filling.

Drop one-third of the dumplings into the boiling water, stirring all the time so that they don't sink and stick to the bottom. >>>

\\

>>> Bring the water back to a boil, then simmer for
2–3 minutes or until the dumplings float back to the
surface. Use a slotted spoon to lift the pierogi onto a
tray and keep warm while you continue to cook the
remaining dumplings.

To serve the dumplings, heat 2 tablespoons of the oil in
a large frying pan over a medium heat, add a few of the
dumplings in a single layer and fry for 2–3 minutes on
each side until golden. Lift out onto a tray, keep warm and
continue with the remaining dumplings, adding
more oil to the pan as needed.

Once all the dumplings are cooked add the remaining oil
to the pan and quickly stir fry the mushrooms until just
tender. Transfer to a bowl, pour over the lemon juice,
scatter with the parsley and serve with the dumplings.

**If you want to cook the pierogi ahead, scoop the
cooked dumplings into a bowl of cold water, before
frying. Leave until cool then drain. They will keep for
a day or two in the fridge, ready to be fried
and served.**

out freaking out!

The growing demand for vegan options on the menu means that more and more restaurants are switching on, stepping up and serving vegan dishes. But what if you don't see that little 'V' mark? Well, you have a few options.

You can scan the menu for an accidentally vegan dish, or something *almost* vegan that you can attempt to 'edit' by requesting a substitution. Be mindful that sometimes dishes will be made with meat or dairy products in advance – or include hidden dairy, such as butter – and can't be changed last minute. But don't be afraid to ask! Be brave, clear and direct. Get the answers you need to feel comfortable.

You can also scan the menu for ingredients. This sounds odd, but if you like the look of half of one dish and an element from another, you could ask the waiter to consult with the kitchen and see if they are willing to create a vegan hybrid (a mixing and matching of ingredients and dishes). Any chef worth his whites will be up for the challenge.

You might feel like you shouldn't have to, but you'll find life a lot easier (and meals out more pleasant) if you take a helpful, amenable and polite approach to exploring the menu and ordering your meal. It would be utterly excellent if every restaurant could cater for every lifestyle and dietary requirement, but the truth is they don't have to. However, if they really don't want to meet you in the middle, you can always vote with your feet and leave.

Of course, if it's a pre-planned night out, you can ring the restaurant ahead of time. Most places will be happy to accommodate with a bit of notice, particularly if you're clear about your needs. And consider more vegan-friendly restaurants, such as those specialising in Indian, Japanese, Thai, Vietnamese or even Mexican.

Ordering Wine

Not all wine is vegan – most is clarified with fining agents like gelatine or egg white. If you're ordering a glass and can't/don't want to ask about its vegan credentials, opt for a 'natural' wine – more and more restaurants and bars are serving these. They are wines made without a fining or filtration process, avoiding the animal products all together. And they often come from forward-thinking, small producers, so you'll be supporting a bijou industry to boot.

Herby Butter Bean & Courgette Stew

SERVES 4

BUTTER BEAN STEW

200g / 7oz dried butter beans,
    soaked overnight, or 2 x
    400g / 14oz cans, drained
    and rinsed
half a bulb of garlic (cut
    a whole bulb horizontally
    across the middle), plus
    4 cloves garlic, peeled
    and halved (use the other
    half of the bulb)
3 bay leaves
2 long strips of lemon zest
100ml / ⅓ cup extra virgin
    olive oil
2 onions, thickly sliced
2 sprigs fresh thyme
4 large courgettes (zucchini),
    thickly sliced
pinch of saffron (optional)
½ tsp fennel seeds (optional)
150ml / ⅔ cup white wine
salt and ground black pepper

FRESH ZOGGHIU TOPPING

handful of parsley, chopped
handful of mint, chopped
3 cloves garlic, peeled
200ml / ¾ cup extra virgin
    olive oil
1 tbsp white wine vinegar

If using dried beans, drain the soaked beans and tip into a large pan. Pour over enough water to cover. Bring to the boil and add the half bulb of garlic, bay leaves and strips of lemon zest (you only need this if using dry beans). Bring back to the boil, then reduce the heat and simmer for 1–1½ hours or until the beans are tender.

While the beans are cooking, make the fresh zogghiu topping. Place the parsley, mint and garlic in the bowl of a food processor and pulse until finely chopped. With the machine running, gradually pour in the olive oil until you have a homogeneous mass. Scrape out into a bowl, stir in the vinegar and season to taste. Set aside.

Continue making the stew. Heat the olive oil in a large pan, then add the sliced onions, the thyme sprigs and peeled garlic clove halves and cook over a low to medium heat for about 10 minutes or until the onions are softened.

Increase the heat, add the courgettes (zucchini) and stir fry for about 10 minutes or until lightly golden. Add the saffron and fennel seeds, if using, and the wine. Let it bubble up, then put a lid on the pan, reduce the heat and cook for 10 minutes more, until the courgettes are tender.

Drain the cooked beans, reserving the cooking water. Discard the garlic, bay and lemon zest. Add the drained butter beans to the pan, along with 3 or 4 ladles of the cooking water. If you are using canned beans instead, add them here, with ladles of plain water. Season to taste with salt and pepper.

Serve the stew with some of the zogghiu drizzled over the top, with the rest on the side.

Black Dahl
/ Nutty Greens

SERVES 6

200g / 1 cup black dahl (urid dahl), split or unsplit

5 tbsp coconut oil

2 tsp black mustard seeds

2 large onions, chopped

4cm / 1½in piece fresh root ginger, very finely grated

3 cloves garlic, crushed

½ tsp chilli powder

½ tsp ground turmeric

½ tsp salt

500ml / 17fl oz almond or other nut milk, or coconut milk

NUTTY GREENS

300g / 10½oz kale, leaves removed from stalk

300g / 10½oz cavolo nero, leaves removed from stalk

pinch of chilli powder or chilli flakes

2 tbsp coconut oil, melted

1 clove garlic, crushed

juice of 1 lemon

50g / ¼ cup tahini (sesame paste)

100g / 1 cup black olives, pitted

100g / 3½oz cashews, chopped

salt

This dish takes time. Linger over it and you'll be rewarded with a rich and tasty curry that will feed many hungry mouths (or just yours over several meals).

In a sieve, rinse the dahl in plenty of cold water until the water runs clear. Tip into a large bowl, cover with water and leave to soak for 8 hours or overnight.

Once ready, drain and rinse the dahl again, tip into a large pan and cover once again with cold water.

Bring to the boil, then simmer, skimming away any scum that rises to the top, for 45 minutes (if using whole urid dahl this may take 1–1½ hours), or until tender.

Heat 2 tablespoons of the coconut oil in a frying pan, add the mustard seeds and let them pop for a minute. Now add the remaining coconut oil and the chopped onions, and cook for 10 minutes, stirring occasionally, until the onions have softened.

Add the ginger and garlic and cook for a further 5 minutes then add the chilli, turmeric and salt. Cook for another minute, stirring all the time.

Drain the dahl leaving just enough water in the pan to cover them (add more fresh water if you drained too much). Add the onion mixture and half of the almond milk. Bring to a simmer, then reduce the heat to very low and cook gently for 1–1½ hours until very thick and creamy, stirring frequently. Check the curry doesn't run dry by topping up with more milk as needed. >>>

>>> When you've used all the milk, use water if necessary.
Check the seasoning.

To make the greens, preheat the oven to 180°C / 360°F /
gas mark 4.

Wash the kale and the cavolo nero and drain. Rip
the leaves into small pieces. Add to a large bowl then
sprinkle with a little salt and a pinch of chilli powder,
and pour over the 2 tablespoons of melted coconut oil.

Toss everything together well, then spread out evenly
on two trays. Place the trays in the oven. Cook for 10
minutes, turning occasionally, until tender and crispy
round the edges. Remove from the oven.

Mix the crushed garlic with the lemon juice and tahini in
a small bowl and drizzle over the cooked greens. Sprinkle
over the olives and chopped cashews and toss well again.

Pile the baked greens on to serving plates and spoon the
dahl on top. You could also serve with rice.

Some beers, wines and spirits use animal-derived products in their filtering and fining processes. Check the label or try a crowd-sourced resource such as www.barnivore.com before cracking open.

Today's craft beer makers (and natural wine makers, page 119) lead the vegan charge. Know your favourites and make these your first choice when you need an easy-order at a busy bar.

Borlotti on Toast

SERVES 4–6

200g / 7oz dried borlotti
  beans, or 250g / 9oz fresh
  podded borlotti beans
  (about 500g / 18oz in their
  pods), or 2 x 400g / 14oz
  cans borlotti beans
5 tbsp extra virgin olive oil,
  plus extra to drizzle
2 cloves garlic, sliced in half
  lengthwise
pinch of chilli flakes
  (optional)
sprig of fresh rosemary
500g / 17½oz ripe tomatoes,
  roughly chopped
salt and freshly ground
  black pepper
sourdough toast, to serve

**If you know someone
who is growing fresh
borlotti, offer to
cook them this, as long
as you can join them!
For a quick supper use
canned beans.**

If using dried borlotti beans, place the beans in a large
bowl and soak in enough water to cover for 6 hours or
overnight. The next day, drain and rinse the soaked beans,
tip into a large pan and again pour over enough water to
cover. Bring to a boil, then reduce the heat and simmer for
about 1–1½ hours, or until tender. Remove from the heat
and leave the beans to cool in their cooking liquid.

If using fresh beans, place the podded beans in a large pan
and pour over enough water to cover. Bring to the boil,
then reduce the heat and simmer for about 30–40 minutes
or until tender. Remove from heat and leave the beans to
cool in their cooking liquid.

If using canned beans, drain and rinse the beans.

Place a large pan over a low heat and add the olive oil.
When the oil is hot, add the halved garlic cloves, chilli
flakes (if using) and rosemary, and fry gently for a minute.

Increase the heat, add the chopped tomatoes, stir and
simmer for 10–15 minutes, or until soft and squishy.

Add the beans to the tomato mixture, adding a couple of
ladles of the bean cooking water. If using canned beans,
add a couple of ladles of water. Bring back to a simmer
and cook for another 10 minutes.

Squash about a third of the beans with the back of a spoon
and season to taste.

Place slices of sourdough toast onto plates, spoon over the
beans and drizzle with a little extra olive oil.

Jollof Rice / Rainbow Slaw

///

SERVES 8

JOLLOF RICE

2 x 400g / 14oz cans chopped
  tomatoes, or 750g / 1lb 10oz
  fresh ripe tomatoes, roughly
  chopped
1–2 Scotch bonnet chillies,
  to taste (remember these
  are fiery!)
2 onions, chopped
3 tbsp vegetable oil
3 cloves garlic, crushed
few sprigs of fresh thyme
1 tbsp smoked paprika
1 tsp ground cinnamon
½ tsp ground ginger
½ tsp ground nutmeg
2 tbsp tomato purée (paste)
500g / 2½ cups basmati or
  long-grain rice
4 bay leaves
1 litre / 4½ cups vegetable
  stock
salt and freshly ground
  black pepper

MUSTARD DRESSING

5cm / 2in piece of fresh
  turmeric, finely grated
1 tsp grainy mustard
juice of 1 orange

100ml / ⅓ cup groundnut
  oil or olive oil, or a mixture
  of both
1 tsp dark brown sugar

RAINBOW SLAW

3 spring onions (scallions),
  finely chopped
200g / 7oz white cabbage,
  very finely sliced
3 carrots (ideally one each of
  orange, purple and yellow),
  cut into thin matchsticks
handful of pomegranate seeds
8 radishes, thinly sliced

VEGETABLE TOPPING

2 tbsp vegetable oil
1 red onion, thinly sliced
1 clove garlic, crushed
1 tbsp all-purpose seasoning
200g / 7oz fine beans,
  roughly chopped
200g / 1½ cups peas, fresh or
  frozen (defrosted if frozen)
200g / 2 cups broad beans
  (fava beans), podded, fresh
  or frozen (defrosted if
  frozen)

**Jollof is never cooked in small quantities,
so it's great for a party, with some leftovers
to take to work in a lunchbox.**

To make the jollof rice, tip the tomatoes, Scotch bonnet(s) and one of the chopped onions into a food processor and whizz until smooth.

Heat the oil in a very large pan. Add the remaining chopped onion, garlic and thyme sprigs and cook for 5 minutes until softened.

Add the spices and cook for a further 2 minutes, then add the tomato purée (paste) and stir fry for another minute. Pour in the puréed tomato mix, bring to the boil, then reduce the heat and simmer for 10 minutes.

Now add the rice, bay leaves and stock. Season with salt and pepper, stir well, and bring back to the boil. Cover the pan tightly with foil, place the lid on top, reduce heat to very low and cook for 20 minutes.

Remove the pan from the heat and let it sit, covered, for 10 minutes, before fluffing up the rice with a fork.

While the rice is cooking, make the slaw. Place all the ingredients for the dressing in the bottom of a large bowl and mix well. Add all the slaw ingredients, season and toss well together. Set aside.

To make the vegetables, heat the oil in a pan, add the sliced red onion and the garlic and cook for 5 minutes to soften. Add the all-purpose seasoning and the chopped fine beans and stir fry for a minute. Raise the heat, then splash in a small cup of water and put the lid on the pan.

Cook for 2–3 minutes, then add the peas and broad (fava) beans and cook for a further 2–3 minutes to heat through.

Serve the jollof rice with the vegetables on top and the slaw alongside.

You don't have to eat alone! When cooking for housemates, go big: a biryani (or jollof, opposite), bean chilli, or ratatouille (see page 64) are all crowd-pleasing winners. If you're going to a friend's house, suggest a theme (Middle Eastern is a safe bet). Or quiz the host on their plan, then offer to bring a dish that fits with the meal – it'll make for a more convivial dining experience. Yes, it might be a faff, but at least you won't go hungry. Cook enough for everyone, and you might even win the other guests over.

Korean Kimchi Pancakes

**MAKES 1 LARGE THICK
PANCAKE OR 4 THIN
PANCAKES**

250g / 9oz Kimchi (see
  page 135)
50g / 6 tbsp rice flour
50g / 6 tbsp plain
  (all-purpose) flour
1 tsp sea salt
200g / 7oz firm tofu
  (beancurd), drained
  and crumbled
100g / 1¾ cups beansprouts
6 spring onions (scallions),
  finely chopped
20g / ¾oz dried seaweed,
  soaked in water for 15
  minutes, then drained
  and chopped
vegetable oil, for frying
sesame seeds, to sprinkle

DIPPING SAUCE
120ml / ½ cup dark soy sauce
6 tbsp toasted sesame oil
4 tbsp rice vinegar
2 tsp chilli flakes (optional)
1 tbsp toasted sesame seeds

Tip the kimchi into a sieve (strainer) over a measuring jug (pitcher), and press down to extract as much juice as possible. Measure the juice and, top it up to 100ml / 3⅓ fl oz with water. Roughly chop the drained kimchi.

Tip the flours into a large bowl with the salt, then whisk in the kimchi juice. Mix in the chopped kimchi, tofu (beancurd), beansprouts, spring onions (scallions) and seaweed and leave to stand for 10 minutes.

Meanwhile, make the dipping sauce. In a small bowl, mix the soy sauce, sesame oil, vinegar, chilli, if using, and sesame seeds.

To cook the pancakes, heat a tablespoon of vegetable oil in a frying pan over a medium-low heat. Ladle in a quarter of the batter and spread it out with the back of a spoon. Cook for 3–5 minutes, until the bottom is crisp and golden, then flip and cook on the other side until that, too, is crisp and golden. Remove from the pan and keep warm while you repeat with the remaining batter, adding a little extra oil to the pan for each pancake.

Alternatively, make one large thick pancake, by adding all the batter to the pan at once. Cook for 10–12 minutes on each side.

Serve the pancake(s) warm, sprinkled with sesame seeds. Serve the dipping sauce on the side.

Kimchi

**MAKES ABOUT 1½ LITRES/
3 PINTS**

1kg/ 2lb 3oz Chinese
  cabbage
4 tbsp sea salt
3 tbsp Korean chilli paste
  (gochujang)
2 tbsp Korean chilli powder
  (gokchu guru)
4 cloves garlic, crushed
4cm / 1½in piece fresh root
  ginger, finely grated
1 tbsp caster (superfine)
  sugar
250g / 9oz mooli (daikon)
  radish, cut into matchsticks
250g / 9oz carrots, peeled and
  cut into matchsticks
4 water chestnuts, cut into
  matchsticks
6 spring onions (scallions),
  cut into matchsticks

**See page 132 for Korean
Kimchi Pancakes.**

Cut the cabbage into quarters and remove the core. Cut the quarters across into 6cm / 2½in pieces and drop into a colander. Add the salt, toss together well and leave for 1½–2 hours, turning once or twice.

Rinse the cabbage under cold running water, drain and dry on dish towels.

In a large bowl, mix together the chilli paste, chilli powder, garlic, ginger and sugar. Add the mooli (daikon), carrots, water chestnuts, spring onions (scallions) and the cabbage and mix together evenly.

Pack the mix into a 3 litre / 6 pint sterilized Kilner jar, pushing the mixture down into the bottom of the jar. Seal and leave at room temperature for 48 hours. Place in the fridge and chill for 4 days before serving. Once a day, burp the jar by opening the lid (it will make a 'phssing' sound) and sealing it again. Keep in the same jar or separate into two or three smaller jars.

The kimchi keeps for at least a month or two, but becomes increasingly stronger in flavour. So it is best used in salads within 2–3 days of making (after the 4 days chilling), then use in cooking.

Banana Semifreddo / Nutty Maple Brittle

\\\\\\\\\\\\\\\\\\\\\\\\\\\\\\\\\\\

SERVES 4

BRITTLE

a little vegetable or coconut
  oil, for greasing
75g / 6 tbsp coconut sugar
125ml / ½ cup maple syrup
pinch of sea salt flakes
50g / 6 tbsp sesame seeds
100g / 1¼ cups toasted flaked
  (slivered) almonds

SEMIFREDDO

200g / 7oz cooked chestnuts
3 tbsp molasses sugar,
  muscovado or dark brown
  sugar
3 tbsp rum
4 ripe bananas
1 tsp vanilla paste or extract
75g / 2⅓oz vegan halva,
  crumbled
2 tbsp hazelnut butter

A semifreddo is a soft scoop ice cream that can be made very quickly, so is perfect for last-minute dinners. The brittle can also be made into a dust to sprinkle on desserts and ice cream, to add to smoothies, or to use as a coating for chocolate truffles (break the brittle into small pieces and whizz to a fine powder in a food processor).

First make the brittle. Grease a baking tray (pan) with a little oil. Mix the coconut sugar, maple syrup and salt together in a pan. Place over a medium-low heat and stir until melted and smooth.

Lower the heat, add the sesame seeds and almonds, and cook for 5 minutes until dark brown and caramelized (be careful not to burn it!). Immediately pour the mixture onto the prepared baking tray, in an even layer. Allow to cool completely. Once cool and hardened, break the brittle into large shards.

To make the semifreddo, tip the chestnuts into the bowl of a food processor with the sugar, and whizz until very smooth. Add the rum, bananas, vanilla, halva and hazelnut butter and whizz until smooth again.

Pour into a small loaf tin or plastic container and place in the freezer. It's ready to eat in an hour or two. If it has frozen too hard to scoop, remove from the freezer and let it soften a little before serving. You can also turn it out on to a plate and slice to serve.

Serve alongside the nut brittle shards.

Apricot, Rose Water & Marzipan Ice Cream

SERVES 6–8

125g / ⅔ cup golden caster (superfine) sugar

500g / 17½oz fresh apricots, stoned and finely chopped

200g / 7oz marzipan, crumbled

300ml / 1¼ cups almond milk

1 tsp rose water

fresh rose petals (optional)

coconut yoghurt (optional)

Pour 125ml / ½ cup water into a pan and add the sugar. Set over a low heat and stir until the sugar has dissolved.

Add the chopped apricots and increase the heat to bring the liquid to the boil, then reduce the heat and cook for about 10 minutes or until tender.

Add the marzipan and cook for a further 1–2 minutes until melted, stirring well. Remove from the heat, then stir in the almond milk and rose water.

Allow to cool for around 45 minutes. Then leave to chill completely in the fridge for 1–2 hours.

Pour the mixture into an ice-cream machine and churn until semi-frozen, then scrape into a plastic container and freeze for 4–6 hours.

Alternatively, pour the mixture into a plastic container, place in the freezer and leave for half an hour. Remove from the freezer, beat the mixture well and return to the freezer. Repeat this every half an hour, beating until smooth. Carry on doing this until the mixture is almost frozen. Then place back in the freezer again and allow to freeze completely.

Serve scooped into small bowls, sprinkled with fresh rose petals and coconut yoghurt if wished.

Pastry

SHORTCRUST PASTRY

200g / 1½ cups plain
  (all-purpose) flour
75g / ¾ cup ground
  almonds
pinch of salt
100g / 3½oz coconut oil
  or coconut butter

SWEET SHORTCRUST PASTRY

200g / 1½ cups plain
  (all-purpose) flour
50g / ½ cup ground
  almonds
pinch of salt
100g / 3½oz coconut oil
  or coconut butter
75g / 6 tbsp light
  muscovado or light
  soft brown sugar
½ tsp vanilla extract

These simple shortcrust pastry recipes will satisfy all of your sweet and savoury tart, pie and quiche needs.

To make the shortcrust pastry, tip the flour, ground almonds and salt into a large bowl. Rub in the coconut oil or butter until the mixture forms fine breadcrumbs. Pour in 3–4 tablespoons water and bring together to form a smooth dough. Wrap and place in the fridge for 30 minutes before rolling out.

To make the sweet shortcrust pastry, tip the flour, ground almonds and salt into a large bowl. Rub in the coconut oil or butter until the mixture forms fine breadcrumbs. Stir in the sugar and vanilla, and add enough water (about 3–4 tablespoons) to form a smooth dough. Wrap and place in the fridge for 30 minutes before rolling out.

To bake the pastry blind, preheat the oven to 190°C / 375°F / gas mark 5. Roll out the dough thinly (to about 3mm / ⅛in thick) and use to line a 23cm / 9in tart tin (pan). Trim off any overhanging pastry or leave a little bit round the edge for a rough finish.

Cut a piece of parchment paper slightly bigger than the tin, place on top of the pastry and fill the tin with baking beans. Place in the oven and bake for 10 minutes, then remove the paper and beans and cook for a further 5–10 minutes or until lightly golden and almost cooked through.

Look out!

Honey

Honey sadly isn't vegan (it is animal-derived). There are sweet alternatives, including: agave, date, maple, malt and brown rice syrups.

Chocolate

A lot of good quality, dark chocolate is vegan, however you should always check the label as dairy products feature in some. Cacao powder, shards or nibs (roasted and broken cacao beans) are vegan and have an intense flavour.

Sweets, sauces... tattoo ink

Animal-derived products can feature in some unexpected edible (and non-edible) products. Look out for gelatine in gummy-like sweets and sauces, and ingredients such as whey, casein, shellac and carmine. And check the ink ingredients with your tattoo parlour before going under the needle!

Chocolate Fridge Roll

2 tbsp coconut butter or
coconut oil
3½ tbsp smooth nut butter
25g / 2 tbsp soft brown sugar
50g / 2½ tbsp golden, maple,
rice or date syrup
½ tsp vanilla paste or extract
300g / 10½oz dark chocolate,
minimum 70% cocoa solids,
broken into pieces
25g / 1oz prunes or dried figs,
pitted and chopped
75g / ½ cup Medjool dates,
pitted and chopped
50g / ⅓ cup mixed dried
berries (cherries, cranberries
or blueberries)
pinch of sea salt flakes
2 tbsp Marsala (optional)
50g / 1¾oz vegan biscuits,
crushed
50g / 3½ tbsp candied orange,
finely chopped
1 knob stem ginger in syrup,
finely chopped
25g / ¼ cup pistachios,
chopped
25g / ¼ cup almonds, toasted
and chopped
25g / 1oz vegan white
chocolate, chopped

This no-bake chocolate roll can also be formed into small balls and rolled in cacao or chopped pistachios to make delicious chocolate truffles.

Place the coconut butter or oil in a large pan with the nut butter, sugar, syrup and vanilla and set over a low heat. When warm and melted together, add the dark chocolate pieces and heat, stirring, until melted.

Remove from the heat and leave to cool slightly, then stir in the rest of the ingredients.

Place a large sheet of parchment paper, about 30cm / 12in long, on a work surface. Scrape the chocolate mixture out of the pan with a spatula and guide it into a line running lengthwise down the middle of the paper.

Roll the paper up over the mixture to create a long cylinder, about 8cm / 3¼in diameter, and twist both ends.

Leave to cool, rolling the cylinder every now and then to create a neat round shape. When cool enough, place in the fridge for 2–3 hours to set completely.

Cut into 2cm / ¾in slices to serve.

Chocolate 'Meringue' Sandwiches

**MAKES 12 INDIVIDUAL
MERINGUES OR 6 MERINGUE
SANDWICHES**

aquafaba – water drained
   from a 400g / 14oz can of
   chickpeas (garbanzo beans)
½ tsp cream of tartar or
   lemon juice
125g / ⅔ cup caster
   (superfine) sugar
½ tsp vanilla extract
   (optional)
100g / 3½oz dark chocolate,
   minimum 70% cocoa solids,
   chopped
6 tbsp Chocolate Hazelnut
   Spread (see page 149)

**Vegan meringues
made with miraculous
aquafaba! Use the
drained chickpeas for
another recipe, such
as Fennel-roasted
Chickpeas (page 87)
or Oven-baked
Ratatouille (page 64).**

Preheat the oven to 120°C / 250°F / gas mark ½. Line two 23 x 32cm / 9 x 12½in baking trays (pans) with parchment paper.

Pour the water drained from the can of chickpeas (garbanzo beans) into a large bowl and use an electric hand-whisk or a stand mixer to whisk for about 5–10 minutes, until it has more than doubled in size and is white and foamy.

Add the cream of tartar or lemon juice and whisk again for another minute. Slowly add the sugar, whisking all the time until the mixture forms stiff, glossy peaks. Stir in the vanilla extract, if using.

Scoop 12 large spoonfuls of the meringue mixture onto the lined baking trays, allowing a little space around them as they will rise slightly. Bake for 2 hours. Do not open the oven! After 2 hours, turn the oven off and leave them to cool completely in the oven before removing.

Bring a pan of water to the boil. Place a heatproof bowl on top and drop the chopped chocolate into the bowl. Remove the pan from the heat and stir the chocolate until melted. Using a teaspoon, drizzle the melted chocolate back and forth across the meringues on the tray. Leave to set.

To make the meringue sandwiches, pull the meringues gently from the paper. Pick up a meringue and scoop a tablespoon of chocolate spread onto its flat base, then place the base of another meringue on top to make a sandwich. Place the sandwich on a serving dish and repeat with the remaining meringues and chocolate spread.

Peanut Butter Lollies / Almond Custard Dip

**MAKES 12 SMALL–
MEDIUM LOLLIES**

LOLLIES

250g / 1¼ cups smooth
   peanut butter
350ml / 1½ cups fresh or
   unsweetened almond milk
3 tbsp light brown sugar
1 vanilla pod (bean), or 1 tsp
   vanilla extract or paste
pinch of salt

ALMOND CUSTARD DIP

500ml / 2¼ cups fresh or
   unsweetened almond milk
1 vanilla pod (bean), or 1 tsp
   vanilla extract or paste
225g / 1¼ cups golden caster
   (superfine) sugar
3 heaped tbsp cornflour
   (cornstarch)

TOPPING

100g / 3½oz vegan white
   chocolate, chopped
75g / ¾ cup chopped toasted
   nuts, Chipotle Cashews
   (page 87) or crushed Nutty
   Maple Brittle (page 136)

To make the lollies, place the peanut butter, almond milk and sugar in a pan. If using, split the vanilla pod (bean) lengthwise and scrape the seeds into the pan, then drop in the pod. Otherwise, add the vanilla extract or paste.

Set the pan over a medium heat, stir until the sugar has dissolved, then remove from the heat, add the salt, stir, and leave to cool completely.

If you used the vanilla pod, remove the pod from the milk mixture then half-fill 12 lolly moulds. Place the remaining lolly mix in the fridge. Freeze the lollies for about 1½ hours or until semi-frozen.

Push a lolly stick upright into the centre of each lolly mould and return to the freezer for another 30 minutes. Top up the lolly moulds with the remaining lolly mix, then return to freezer for at least 4 hours or overnight to freeze until completely solid.

To make the custard, pour 400ml / 1¾ cups of the almond milk into a pan. If using, split the vanilla pod lengthwise and scrape the seeds into the pan, then drop in the pod. Otherwise, add the vanilla extract or paste.

Meanwhile, tip the sugar and cornflour (cornstarch) into a large bowl, pour in the remaining milk and whisk until blended.

Heat the milk, and when just about to boil, pour in the cornflour mix, whisking all the time. Cook, stirring, until smooth and thickened. >>>

>>> Pour the custard back into the bowl and cover the surface with parchment paper or cling film (plastic wrap) to stop a skin from forming. Leave to cool.

To melt the chocolate for the topping. Bring a small pan of water to the boil, then reduce to a simmer. Place a heatproof bowl on top of the pan and tip the chopped chocolate into the bowl. Remove the pan from the heat and stir until melted.

Place the chopped nuts, fried cashews, or crushed brittle in a small bowl.

Remove the lollies from the freezer, take them out of their moulds and roll each lolly into the melted chocolate, then into the chopped nuts. Place the lollies back in the moulds (or on a tray) back in the freezer while you reheat the custard over a low-medium heat.

Serve the lollies with the warm custard to dip into. They will keep for up to a week in the freezer.

Chocolate Hazelnut Spread / Matcha Almond Milk / Coconut Snow

Chocolate Hazelnut Spread

////////////////////////////////

**MAKES 2 X 300ML /
10FL OZ JARS**

150g / 1¼ cups blanched
  hazelnuts
400ml / 14fl oz hazelnut milk
225g / 8oz dark chocolate,
  minimum 70% cocoa solids,
  roughly chopped
50g / 5 tbsp golden caster
  (superfine) sugar or 5 tbsp
  date or maple syrup
½ tsp vanilla extract
pinch of salt

Preheat the oven to 180°C / 360°F / gas mark 4.

Spread out the nuts in a single layer on a baking tray (pan). Bake for about 12–15 minutes until golden, then remove from the oven and allow to cool.

Tip the cooled roasted nuts into the bowl of a food processor and whizz until you have a very smooth paste (this may take a while).

Meanwhile, pour the milk into a pan, add the chopped chocolate and sugar or syrup. Set over a very low heat and stir continuously until melted and smooth (don't let it burn!). Stir in the vanilla and salt.

With the food processor running, pour the melted chocolate milk mixture into the hazelnut paste and whizz until smooth. Pour into jars, allow to cool, then chill until set.

Keeps for about a week in the fridge.

Matcha Almond Milk

300ml / 1¼ cups almond milk or other nut milk
1 tbsp date, rice or maple syrup, or to taste
½ tsp matcha powder
a spoonful of Coconut Snow (below)

To make the matcha almond milk, pour the nut milk into a blender with the syrup and the matcha and whizz well until very smooth and frothy.

Spoon in some coconut snow and stir, just before serving.

Serve with the chocolate hazelnut spread on sourdough toast.

Coconut Snow

1 quantity Fresh Coconut Milk (page 10) or a 400ml / 14fl oz can coconut milk

Pour the coconut milk into a container with 300ml / 1¼ cups cold water and freeze until solid. (This will take a few hours at least. It needs to be very hard, so preferably leave overnight.)

Remove the frozen coconut milk from the freezer and leave at room temperature for about 15 minutes to soften slightly.

Break up the frozen coconut milk, drop the pieces into the bowl of a food processor, and whizz to create a powder-like snow. Return the snow to the freezer for 1–2 hours.

Best used within a week or two.

You don't have
to feel confused.
If in doubt about
a product's vegan
credentials, consult
a source such as
www.peta.org.
It compiles lists
of vegan-friendly
fashion retailers,
beauty brands, and
animal cruelty-free
businesses, which
can help you to make
the choices you feel
comfortable with in
every part of life.

You don't have
to feel alone.
There are vegan
societies, clubs,
meet-ups and
even dating
apps that can
bring you closer
to likeminded
people. Find
them, join in,
feel the

love.

Live by your own rules when it comes to your diet and lifestyle, after all, it is yours. How possible and practical it is to adopt veganism in every aspect of life is personal to you and might evolve over time; don't let anyone make you feel guilty or defensive about a decision they feel doesn't fit the vegan label (or is 'awkward' or 'difficult'). By choosing to be a vegan, you are being considerate to the planet and compassionate towards animals. Remember to be kind to yourself, too.

No apologies, no excuses. Just be true to you.

\\

Publishing Director Sarah Lavelle
Commissioning Editor Zena Alkayat
Design Manager Claire Rochford
Art Direction / Design Maeve Bargman
Cover Design Luke Bird
Photographer Kim Lightbody
Props Stylist Rachel Vere
Food Stylist Annie Nichols
Production Director Vincent Smith
Production Controller Nikolaus Ginelli

Published in 2018 by Quadrille,
an imprint of Hardie Grant Publishing

Quadrille
52–54 Southwark Street
London SE1 1UN
quadrille.com

ISBN 978 1 78713 274 0

Printed in China